Getting Started

with

Windows® 3.1

Wiley PC Companions

Stern/Stern: GETTING STARTED WITH STRUCTURED BASIC, Second Edition
Murphy: GETTING STARTED WITH DOS 5.0
Russakoff: GETTING STARTED WITH WINDOWS 3.1
Kronstadt/Sachs: DISCOVERING MICROSOFT WORKS 2.0
Murphy: GETTING STARTED WITH WORDPERFECT 4.2/5.0**
Murphy: GETTING STARTED WITH WORDPERFECT 5.1
Murphy/Potter: GETTING STARTED WITH LOTUS 1-2-3, RELEASE 2.2
Farrell: GETTING STARTED WITH LOTUS 1-2-3, RELEASE 2.3
Murphy: GETTING STARTED WITH QUATTRO**
Arnolds/Hammonds/Isham: GETTING STARTED WITH dBASE III PLUS**
Gaylord: GETTING STARTED WITH dBASE IV
Wiley: EXPLORING DOS, WORDPERFECT 5.1, LOTUS 1-2-3 (RELEASE 2.2), AND dBASE III PLUS

** Educational version software available

Wiley Macintosh Companions

Abernethy, Nanney and Porter: EXPLORING MACINTOSH: Concepts In Visually Oriented Computing
Nanney, Porter and Abernethy: EXPLORING MICROSOFT WORKS 2.0--Macintosh

Getting Started with Windows® 3.1

Sylvia Russakoff
Pace Computer Learning Center
Pace University

Babette Kronstadt
David Sachs
Consulting Editors
Pace Computer Learning Center
Pace University

John Wiley and Sons, Inc.
New York Chichester Brisbane Toronto Singapore

Trademark Acknowledgments:

IBM is a registered trademark of International Business Machines Corporation
Windows is a registered trademark of Microsoft Corporation

ISBN 0-471-58617-X

Printed in the United States of America

10 9 8 7 6 5 4 3

CONTENTS

Getting Started with Windows 3.1

Introduction

Lesson 1 The Windows Environment: Part I

Lesson 2 The Windows Environment: Part II

Lesson 3 The Program Manager

Lesson 4 Using Windows Help

Lesson 5 Using Windows Write

Lesson 6 Exploring Windows Accesories

Lesson 7 Sharing Data Among Applications

Lesson 8 Using the File Manager

Lesson 9 Using the Control Panel

Lesson 10 Creating A New Program Group

Lesson 11 Creating Special Links Between Applications

Appendix B: Installing Windows and Printing in Windows

Appendix C: Using Non-Windows Applications

PREFACE

Many experts feel that the advent of Windows, a product of Microsoft Corporation, is the most exciting development in software in recent years. Windows provides a graphical user interface, a platform for running both Windows and DOS applications, the opportunity to do multitask applications, a selection of convenient accessories, and much, much more. Millions of copies have been sold, and users in both office and home environments are enjoying its manifold advantages. Windows 3.1 represents the latest version of this program.

This book provides a step-by-step introduction to the terminology, concepts, and techniques needed in order to use Windows 3.1. Lessons 1 and 2 introduce you to the Windows environment. Lessons 3 through 5 introduce the Windows Program Manager, Help function, and word processor. Lessons 6 and 7 introduce the remaining Windows accessories. Lessons 8 through 11 and the Appendices introduce various advanced topics.

Acknowledgments

I wish to express my thanks and appreciation to my colleagues at the Pace University Computer Learning Center, who have given me the time to write this book, and the support and help I needed in doing so. Babette Kronstadt has read each lesson and contributed her ideas and advice. Barbara Farrell worked through the exercises and helped me to clarify them and sharpen their focus. My thanks to Lynn Bacon, whose artistic sense and skills guided the book's appearance. I also appreciate the cooperation and concern of Andrea Bryant of John Wiley & Sons, Inc. Finally, my thanks to my daughter Nina, whose summer vacation largely consisted of word processing, and without whom this book could not have been completed.

I
Introduction

Hardware Needed

- IBM AT/PS2 or compatible microcomputer
- 640K conventional memory and *at least* 256K, preferably 1024K extended memory
- Hard drive with *at least* 6 MB, preferably 9 MB free
- At least one floppy disk drive

Software Needed

- IBM-DOS or MS-DOS 3.1 or later
- Windows 3.1
- Student Data disk (supplied with this book)

Windows 3.1

Windows 3.1 offers the user a new, multifeatured environment in which to operate a personal computer. With Windows, Microsoft Corporation has revolutionized the way people set up their PCs, organize their software, and run the programs they need. Windows 3.1 represents the latest and most advanced version of Windows. Some of its important features are listed below:

1. Windows employs a *graphical user interface* (GUI). In addition to placing commands and instructions onscreen as text, Windows contains small pictures called *icons*, which represent programs, devices, documents, and commands. To select an icon for use, you click on it with a device called a "mouse."

2. Windows uses the desktop metaphor. Each task you perform takes place in its own window, and all windows can be sized and arranged on the screen just as you would arrange the papers on your desk.

3. Windows comes with a complete set of accessories to help you organize your work: a calculator, cardfile, calendar, notepad, and more.

4. Windows allows you to run programs created especially for its environment (Windows applications), and also conventional programs created to run under DOS (non-Windows applications). It allows you to open more than one program from your hard disk at a time, and switch quickly and easily from one program to another. If you have sufficient memory, Windows lets you actually process data from two different applications at the same time. This is called multitasking.

5. All Windows applications share the same "look" and "feel." Because they have a common appearance and mode of operation, once you learn the basics—managing windows, saving, retrieving, and printing files—you can use the same techniques in all programs created for Windows.

6. All Windows applications share the same setup information. Once you have configured your mouse, printers, and other devices during the Windows setup, they are available for all Windows programs.

7. Windows permits easy transfer of data between applications. Besides copying and moving data, you can create special links between applications that let you update more than one file at a time.

Using This Book

The advantages of Windows are not enjoyed without effort.
More than other software applications, learning Windows often leads to an initial period of confusion and frustration. The new Windows user is faced with a myriad of choices and screens (See Figure I-1). Using the mouse may prove a challenge. Often, it seems to the user that windows open and close on their own, sometimes disappearing without warning!

Our advice—press on! Typically, once the initial resistance and frustration are overcome, users appreciate the power and fun of Windows. Read each lesson carefully, more than once if necessary. Look back to earlier lessons if you forget a definition or an instruction. We think you will find the effort well worthwhile.

This book will introduce you to the basic information you need to understand and use Windows 3.1. There will be numerous exercises to help you practice what you are learning. Although Windows 3.1 can be used with many kinds of software—both Windows and non-Windows applications—the exercises will require only the applications that are included with Windows 3.1 and files that you will find on the Student Data disk included with this book.

Each exercise consists of numbered instructions. Text you are expected to type will be printed in **bold** type. Most chapters will conclude with Review Exercises, which contain suggestions and hints rather than detailed instructions. At the end of the book you will find five Projects, which are designed to help you organize and assimilate the knowledge you have acquired.

You will be using the Control (CTRL), Alternate (ALT), and Function keys (F1 through F12) in combination with normal typing keys to carry out the instructions in this book.

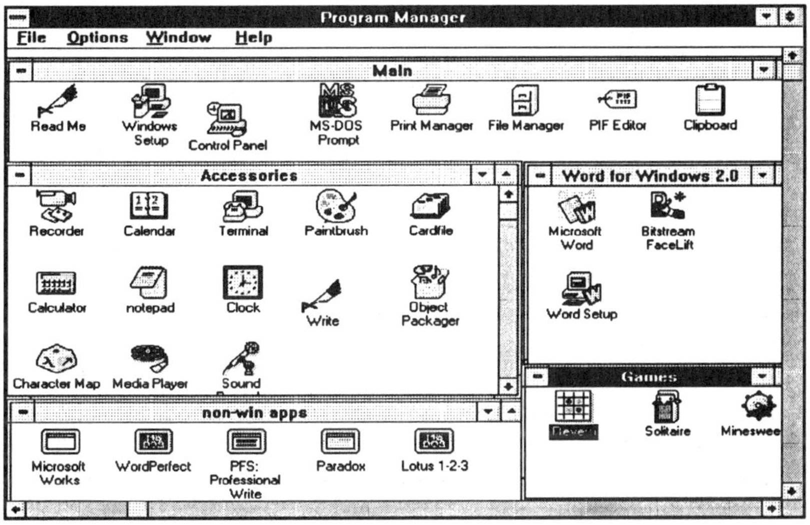

Figure I-1: Windows 3.1 *(one of many possible screens)*

Starting Windows

Windows is usually started either from the DOS prompt or by selecting it from a customized menu. Often a personal computer using Windows is set up so that Windows will open automatically as part of the start-up routine (through a command in the AUTOEXEC.BAT file.) If the Windows installation procedure has been followed, Windows can be loaded by typing: **win**. *If this command does not work, check any menus that appear on your screen or ask your instructor for help.*

To start Windows from the DOS prompt,

1. Turn on your computer and monitor.
2. At the C:\ prompt, type: **win**.
3. Press ENTER.

Modes of Operation

Windows 3.1 can operate on a wide range of personal computers. However, computer systems with less memory (RAM) and less powerful processors cannot take full advantage of Windows' capabilities. When you start Windows, it looks at your hardware capacity, and depending on what it finds, operates in either of two modes:

Standard Mode

1. The normal operating mode for running Windows.
2. Requires an 80286 processor (or higher), 640K conventional memory, and 256K extended memory.
3. Lets you switch among Windows and non-Windows applications.
4. Provides access to extended memory.

386 Enhanced Mode

1. Requires an 80386 processor (or higher), 640K conventional memory, and 1024K extended memory.
2. Lets you switch between Windows and non-Windows applications and multi-task non-windows applications.
3. Lets you use more memory than is actually physically available (by using the "virtual memory" capabilities of the 386 processor).

Windows 3.0 can be used with computers with an 8086 processor and 640K memory. In that situation, Windows 3.0 will operate in Real Mode, which has more limited capabilities than either standard or enhanced mode.

Microsoft advises that a 386 machine with less than 4MB of memory may run Windows slowly. As long as you are not planning to run non-Windows applications, Windows will run faster in standard mode. To run Windows and specify standard mode, type:......**win /s**. To run Windows and specify enhanced mode, type:.....**win /e**. We will learn more about standard and enhanced modes in a later lesson.

1

The Windows Environment Part I

The objectives of this lesson are to

- Define the Windows environment
- Understanding basic Windows terminology
- Identify the elements of the Program Manager window
- Use the mouse

Note: One of the difficulties in working with Windows is the number of different ways a screen can be displayed. Although a student may follow instructions correctly, the screen that appears may not resemble our illustration. In addition, Windows does not always return to the same default setting or screen arrangement, but instead may return to the way a screen was left at its last use. We have tried to give instructions to encompass these situations, but if you have trouble, ask your instructor for help.

The Windows Environment

The Windows environment includes the terminology and procedures you need to know in order to *begin* to use Windows. Windows is sometimes confusing to beginners because of the vast number of choices to make and the various, often unexpected screen transformations that occur. Lessons 1 and 2 teach you how to control and manage the Windows environment. You will find that once you have mastered the material in these lessons you will feel more confident and ready to explore further.

Basic Terms

Windows has its own vocabulary. Here are some basic terms you need to know.

1. **Window.** An area enclosed within a frame where an application can run, or a document can be displayed. Every activity you carry out will take place within a window.

2. **Desktop.** Unenclosed background area behind a window.

3. **Applications.** A computer program which can run in the Windows environment. Applications designed to be used with Windows, like the Notepad and Cardfile, are called Windows Applications. Some applications, like WordPerfect and Lotus 1-2-3 are non-Windows Applications which can be used in the Windows environment.

4. **Menu.** A horizontal list of commands listed across the upper part of a window.

5. **Application Window**. A window which displays an application, for example Paintbrush or Windows Write. An application window always contains a menu.

6. **Document Window**. A window which does not contain a menu.

7. **Icon**. A picture symbol that can represent an application, document, file or drive. By manipulating the icon you can control the entity it represents.

8. **Control menu box**. A small gray box in the upper left corner of *every* window. It controls the size of the window, can be used to switch to another application, and can be used to close the window.

9. **Active**. When a window or icon is active, the bar across its top (the title bar) changes to a more vivid color. You cannot work with a window or its contents unless it is active.

10. **Mouse**. A small, hand-held device used to give commands within Windows. The mouse will make your work easier and faster. The mouse is represented on your screen by the *mouse pointer*. The pointer will change shape, depending on the kind of task you are engaged in.

We will begin our lesson by starting Windows 3.1 and making the initial screen resemble Figure 1-1.

To open Windows and see the Program Manager,

1. Open Windows 3.1, following the procedure used in the Introduction (hint: type **win** at the c:\ prompt and press ENTER).

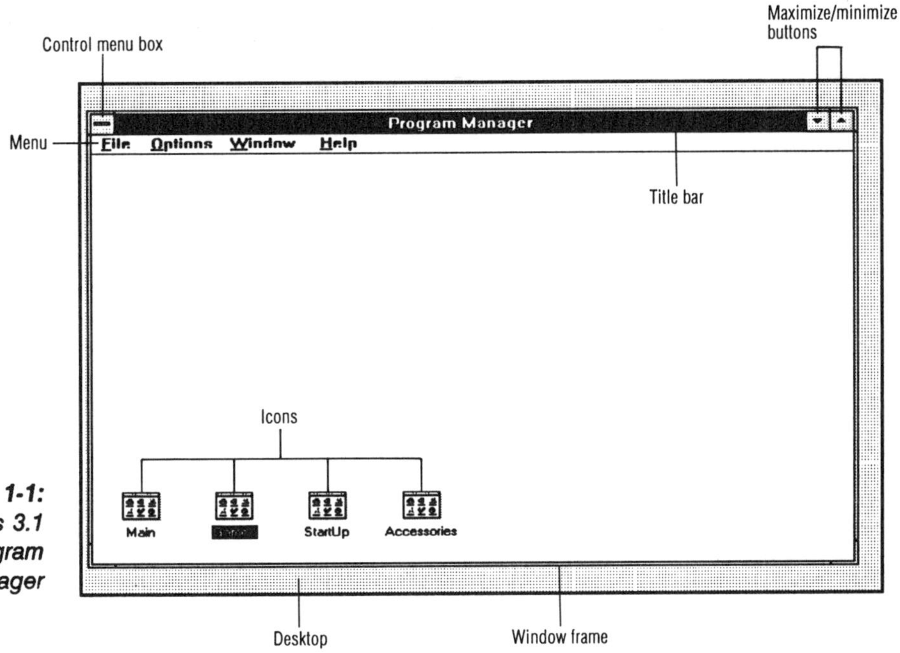

Figure 1-1: *Windows 3.1 Program Manager*

When you start Windows, the application that opens immediately is called the Program Manager. The Program Manager is the application that organizes and runs the entire Windows environment. You will learn about it in more detail in Lesson 3. The Program Manager always appears on your screen when you open Windows; however it may not look like Figure 1-1 (above).

The appearance of The Program Manager depends on whether its own window and the windows it contains are open or closed, and on the software installed with Windows on your PC.

Sometimes the Program Manager appears as a small icon (picture) at the bottom of the screen. *If your screen looks like Figure 1-2, follow these directions*:

To open the Program Manager icon,

1. Hold down the ALT key and press the SPACEBAR.
2. Press ENTER.

It is possible that your screen may show the Program Manager containing a number of open windows. For now, we want to close any open windows inside the Program Manager. *If your screen resembles Figure 1-3, follow these directions*:

To close open windows inside the Program Manager,

1. Press CTRL+F4 repeatedly until all windows have closed.
2. You will now see a group of icons inside the Program Manager.

Note: If a window does not close, press CTRL+TAB until its top and frame turn color. The color change means that the window is active and it will close when you press CTRL+F4. If you still cannot close an open window inside the Program Manager, ask your instructor for help.

Figure 1-2: *The Program Manager as an Icon*

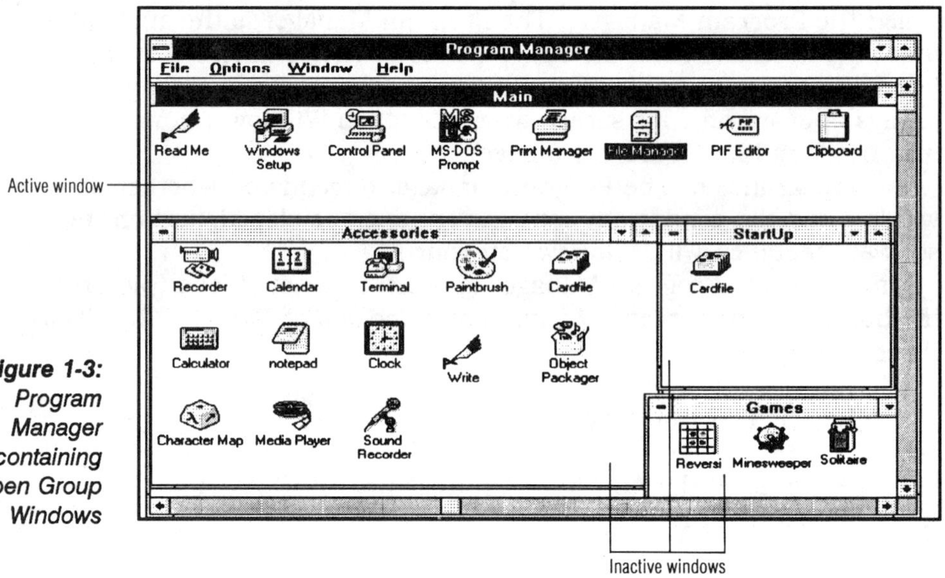

Figure 1-3: *Program Manager containing Open Group Windows*

At this point your screen should look like Figure 1-1: the Program Manager window will be open and will contain a group of icons. The number of icons you see inside the Program Manager depends on the software you have available and the choices made during the Windows installation (for more information on installing Windows, see Appendix B).

The Parts of a Window

In Windows, every activity takes place in a window. Once you are familiar with the parts of a window and how each works, you can apply this knowledge throughout the Windows environment. The Program Manager window contains the basic window elements, as seen in Figure 1-1.

1. **Title Bar.** Shows the name of the application or document.

2. **Control Menu Box.** In the upper left corner of *every* window. It contains an icon that looks like a minus sign. When opened, you see the control menu, which contains commands that affect the size and location of the window and allow you to close the window.

3. **Maximize/Minimize Restore Buttons.** Icons in the upper right corner of almost every window. The minimize button (▾) is a triangle pointing down. It shrinks the window to an icon. The maximize button (▴) is a triangle pointing up. It enlarges the window to fill the entire screen. When a window is maximized, the maximize button is replaced by the restore icon, which contains two triangles. The restore icon returns the window to its original size, which is neither maximized nor minimized.

4. **Menu Bar.** Appears only if the window belongs to an application. The menu bar displays the menus available for the application. Through the menus, you give the commands necessary to work in your application.

5. **Window Frame.** Every window is surrounded by a frame. The frame size can be changed with either the mouse or cursor keys.

Using the Mouse

Although you can use Windows without a mouse, using one will speed up your work. In addition, it is fun! We will mention shortcut keys occasionally, when they are easier or faster than the mouse. In Appendix D, you will find a complete list of shortcut key combinations.

Mouse Actions

There are four mouse actions to learn:

Pointing. Moving the mouse so that the pointer *touches* the text or icon of your choice.

Clicking. Lightly pressing and releasing the *left* mouse button (the right mouse button is rarely used in Windows).

1. Point to the word **Window** on the menu bar and click to open the menu.
2. Point to any empty spot on the screen outside the menu, and click to close the menu.
3. Point to the icon called **Main** in the Program Manager and click to make the icon active and open its control menu.
4. Point to empty space anywhere on the screen and click to close the menu. The icon will remain active.

Double-Clicking. Rapidly pressing and releasing the left mouse button twice *without jiggling the mouse.*

Dragging. Clicking and moving the mouse *while the left button is kept down.* When you have dragged the object to the location of your choice, release the button.

1. Point to the icon called **Games** in the Program Manager. Drag it to another spot in the Program Manager window.
2. Point to the word **Help** on the menu bar and click to open the menu.
3. Click on **How to Use Help**. A window will open.
4. Double-click on the control menu box (icon that looks like a minus sign in the upper left corner of the Help screen). The window will close and you will return to the Program Manager.

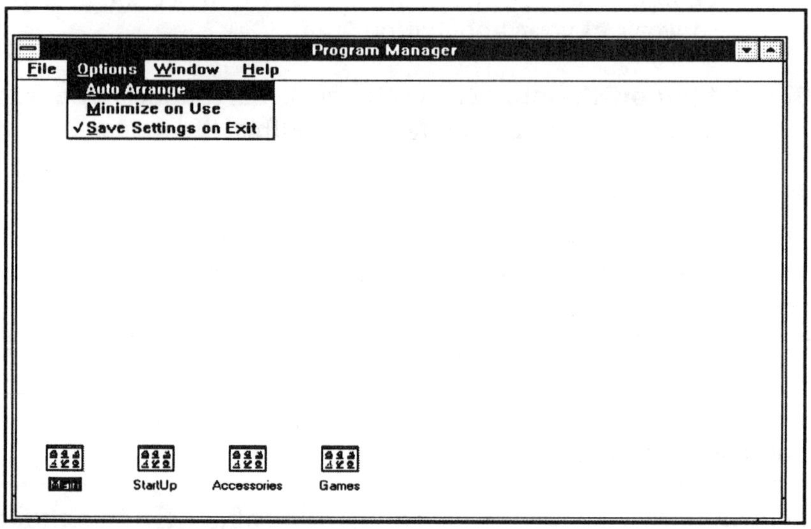

Figure 1-4: An Open Menu

Using the Menus

Now that we have begun to look at menus, you are likely to notice that some choices are listed in dark type and some in light type. Any menu item printed in light type is not available.

To open a menu,

1. Point to the Options menu and click (See Figure 1-4).

To close a menu,

1. Close the Options menu by pointing to empty space anywhere on the screen and clicking.

To choose an item from a menu,

1. Open the Help menu, and click About Program Manager. After reading the display, click on OK.

Using the Mouse to Control a Window

Many of the icons (pictures) that you see on your Windows screen can be opened into windows. Knowing how to do this is an important basic task you must learn. The easiest way to open an icon into a window is to double-click on the icon.

When you double-click on an icon to open it into a window, the window that opens will be active. The newly opened window will sometimes display its own icons inside.

To open an icon into a window,

1. Double-click on the icon titled **Main**.

The icon opens into a window, and you can see its icons (See Figure 1-5).

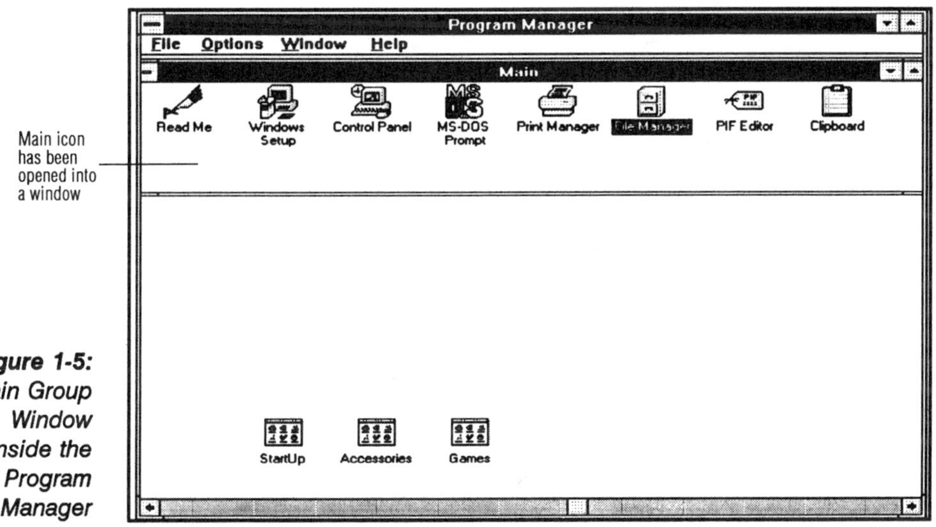

Figure 1-5: *Main Group Window inside the Program Manager*

Now that you have opened a window, you need to know how to close it.

To close a window,

1. Double-click on the control menu box of the Main window.

2. An *alternate* method of closing the window is to click on the control menu box and click on the word Close.
The window closes and returns to an icon.

Besides opening and closing windows, you can also use the mouse to maximize (expand to full screen size) and minimize (shrink to an icon) any window.

To maximize a window,

1. Click on the maximize button (▲), which is the triangle facing up in the upper right corner of the Program Manager.
2. To restore the Program Manager to its former size, click on the restore button (the double triangle that has replaced the maximize button).

To minimize a window,

1. Click on the minimize button (▼), which is the triangle facing down. The Program Manager now appears as an icon.
2. To restore the Program Manager, double-click on its icon.

2

The Windows Environment Part II

The objectives of this lesson are to

- Open and close applications
- Change the size and placement of windows
- Use dialog boxes

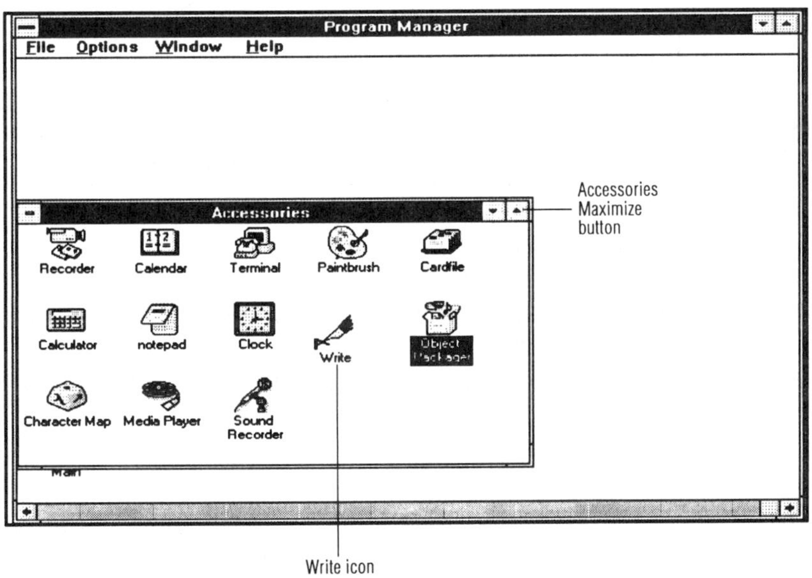

***Figure 2-1:** The Accessories Window*

Using the Mouse to Control an Application

Once you can use your mouse to control a window, you can use the same techniques to open and close applications (programs). If the icon for the application you want to run is not on your screen, you will first need to open the window in which it is found. In the following example, we will open and close the application called **Windows Write**, a word processing program that is one of the Windows Accessories. To reach the **Write** icon, we first have to open the **Accessories** window.

To open the Windows Write application,

1. Double-click on the **Accessories** icon to open it (see Figure 2-1).
2. Look in the window for the icon titled **Write.** Double-click on it (see Figure 2-2).

If you cannot see the Write icon, enlarge the Accessories window by clicking on the maximize button (triangle pointing up (▲) in the upper right corner).

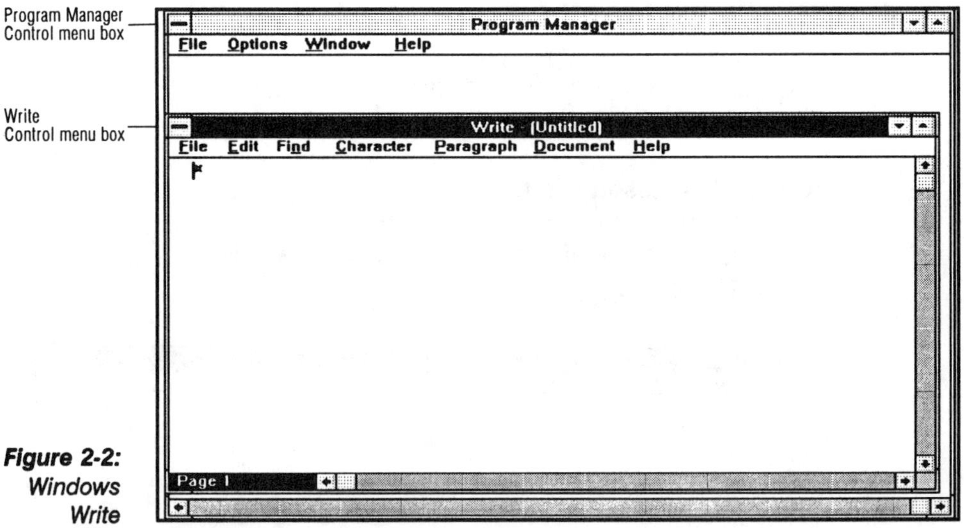

Figure 2-2: *Windows Write*

To close the Windows Write application,

1. Double-click on the Write control menu box (hint: upper left corner of the Write window).
2. An alternate method of closing the application is to click on the File menu and choose Exit.

Dialog Boxes

Dialog boxes help you give more complicated commands to Windows. By now, you have had some experience with Windows menus. You may have noticed that some menu items are followed by a set of three dots. The dots are called an ellipsis. The ellipsis appears after commands that cannot be carried out without further information. When you choose such a command, Windows automatically opens a *dialog box*, in which you can specify your command more fully. Dialog boxes contain different elements within a single frame (see Figure 2-3).

Dialog Box Elements

1. **Option Buttons.** Round buttons, only one of which may be selected at a time. To select, click on the option of your choice.

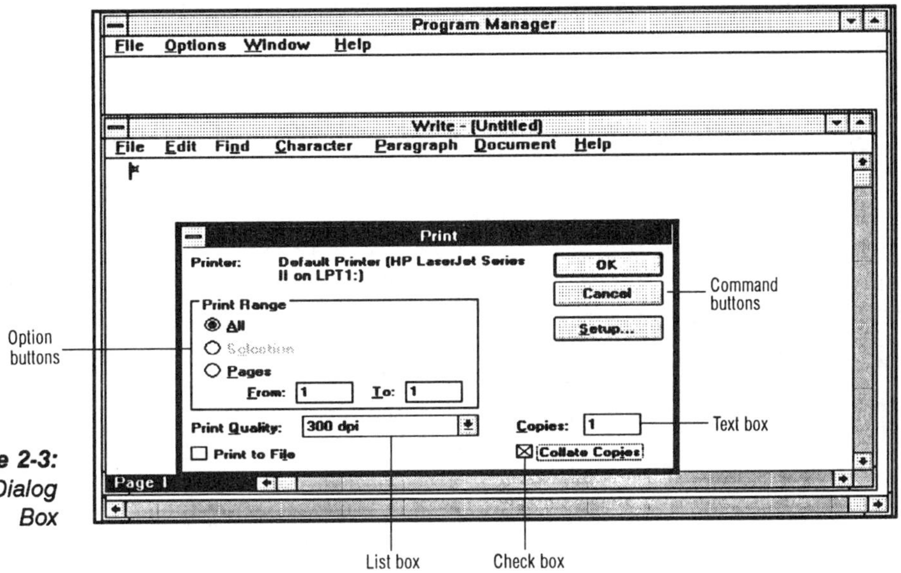

***Figure 2-3:** A Dialog Box*

2. **Check Boxes.** Square boxes. You may select as many as you wish. To select or deselect, click on the box.
3. **Text Boxes.** A blinking cursor in a box indicates that the box is meant to contain text and is ready to be used. Type the text you want in the box. If a text box does not contain a blinking cursor, click in the box and then begin to type. When the mouse pointer touches a text box, it changes shape from a single-headed arrow to a slender **I**.
4. **List Boxes.** Contains a list of choices. Pick the one you want by clicking on it. If the list box has a down arrow at the right edge, you can *open* it to see more choices by clicking on the arrow.
5. **Command Buttons.** Gray boxes that appear on the right or bottom of your dialog box. Click on OK to carry out the instructions *or* press ENTER. Click on Cancel to cancel the box *or* press ESC.

To use a dialog box,

1. Open Write (hint: the Write icon is in the Accessories window).
2. Point to the File menu and click to open it.
3. Click on **Print...** The Print dialog box will open.
4. Look at the option buttons in the Print Range area. Click on the **Pages** button.
5. Open the **Print Quality** list box by clicking on the down arrow. Click on one of the choices.

6. Click on the check box marked **Print to File** to select it. Click again to deselect.
7. Click on the text box marked **Copies**. Type the number **2** in the box and delete the **1.**
8. Click on the **Cancel** command button to cancel the dialog box.
9. Close Write (hint: choose File and Exit).
10. Close the Accessories window.

Moving and Sizing Windows

Now that you are used to opening and closing windows you may have noticed that they do not always open in a convenient place. Sometimes one window blocks another partially or completely. You can control the size of any window by adjusting its frame with your mouse. You can move a window anywhere on the desktop by using your mouse to drag it to a new location.

To move the Program Manager window,

1. Click on the Program Manager title bar and drag the window to a new location. Remember, you *must* click on the title bar before you drag the window, or the window will not move.
2. Drag the Program Manager again, making sure that all four sides of the window frame are visible.

You can size a window by positioning the mouse pointer anywhere on the window frame and dragging the frame.

To size the Program Manager window,

1. Position the mouse pointer on the right frame of the Program Manager.
2. When the pointer changes to a two-headed arrow, click and then drag the frame to the right or left. This will shrink or widen the window. Be sure to move your cursor slowly. The two-headed arrow will only be visible when your cursor is on the window frame.
3. Position the pointer on the top of the frame and drag it up or down.
4. Position the pointer on one of the four corners and notice that the two-headed arrow is now diagonal. Dragging now changes the length and width at the same time.
5. Leave the window centered, filling about 3/4 of the screen.

Leaving Windows

To close Windows, you must close the Program Manager. You close the Program Manager just as you would any other window: by double-clicking on its control menu box or by opening the control menu and choosing Close.

To close Windows,

1. Double-click the control menu box of Windows.
2. In the **Exit** dialog box, click on OK.

Review Exercises

1. Open Windows by following the method described in the text, or from a menu on your computer.
2. Arrange the Program Manager as an open window containing only icons.
3. Move the Program Manager to different locations around the desktop, and finally center it.
4. Maximize the Program Manager, then minimize it, then restore it to its original size.
5. Open the Main window from its icon.
6. Open the icon called Control Panel. Open the Settings menu and choose Date/Time... Change the settings only if they are not correct. Click on OK.
7. Resize the Control Panel window so that it is very small and then close it.
8. Resize the Main window, making it as large as you can. Make it smaller again, then close it.
9. Close any other open windows inside the Program Manager and then close Windows.

3
The Program Manager

The objectives of this lesson are to

- Define the Program Manager
- Understand Program Groups
- Open and Close program group windows
- Use the Cascade and Tile commands
- Use the Task List

Note: Before you begin your work in this chapter, turn on your computer and start Windows. If your screen does not match Figure 3-1, follow the directions in Lesson 1.

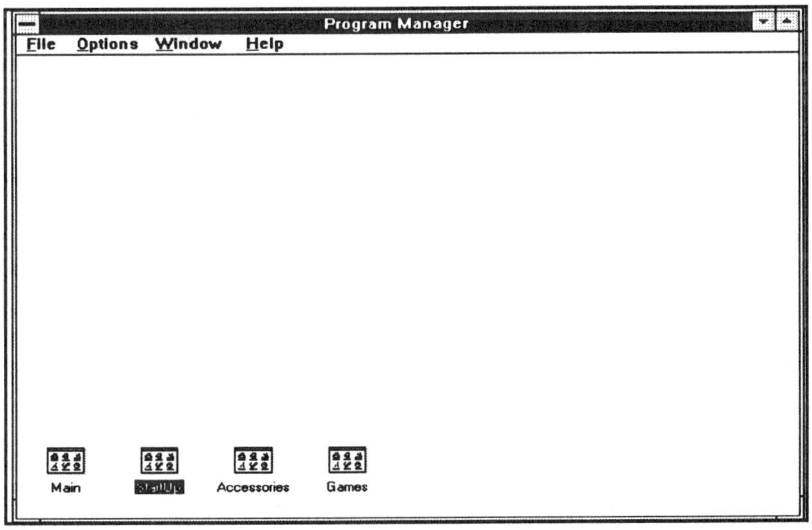

Figure 3-1: *Windows 3.1 Program Manager*

The Program Manager

As we learned in Lesson 1, whenever you are running Windows the Program Manager is open. But what role does the Program Manager play in the organization and use of Windows?

The Program Manager is an application—the umbrella or master program under which all other applications run in Windows. These applications are organized in *program groups*, which are represented by the icons you see inside the Program Manager window. When you open one of these icons, as you did in the last lesson, you will see a *program group window*, displaying an icon for each application it contains.

Four of the program groups, **Main, Accessories, Games,** and **Startup**, are defined by Windows 3.1. The first three contain applications assigned by Windows, but the fourth, Startup, will remain empty until you add applications to it. All Windows users will have these groups.

1. **Main.** Contains applications that help you manage Windows and run your programs efficiently.
2. **Accessories.** Contains applications to help you organize your job activities.
3. **Games.** For those times when you need a break. Also useful for improving your control with the mouse!
4. **Startup.** Any applications you add to this group will open automatically when you open Windows.

In addition, other program groups are created by the user and contain icons for various Windows or non-Windows applications.

Therefore, except for Main, Games, Accessories, and Startup, two Windows users may have distinctly different program groups and applications.

Unless you are using Windows from a computer network, you can easily move or copy an application from one program group to another, as we will do in Lesson 9. For more information about user-created groups, see Lesson 9 and the Appendix (installing Windows 3.1).

Opening Program Group Windows

In Lesson 1 we opened the Accessories group window and the Main group window. It was easy to see the icon for each one inside the Program Manager. However, sometimes it is impossible to open a program group this way because the icon may be blocked by a window and therefore not visible. Instead, you can always open a program group window from the Window menu.

To see a list of program groups on your computer,

1. Click on the Window menu. You will see a numbered list of all your program groups (see Figure 3-2).

To Open the Games program group,

1. Click on **Games**.

Don't forget that as long as the icon is visible, you can still open any group window by double-clicking on its icon.

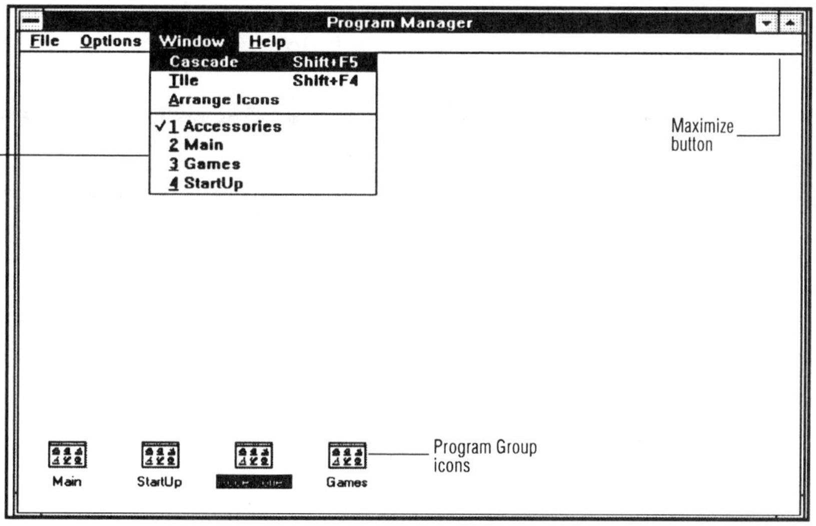

Figure 3-2: *Windows 3.1 Program Groups*

Using the Cascade and Tile Commands

When you look at the group window on your screen (Games), you will notice that it does not have a menu. Windows that do not contain menus are called *document windows* and are controlled through the application under which they run. All group windows are controlled through the Program Manager. Like other windows, group windows may partially or completely block each other. The *Cascade* and *Tile* commands on the Window menu let you arrange your document windows so that none is hidden. The Cascade command arranges your windows so that the title bar of each is visible. The Tile command arranges the windows so that they are sized equally within the Program Manager.

To Cascade a group of document windows,

1. Open the Games, Accessories, and Main windows (hint: use the Window menu).
2. Maximize the Program Manager (hint: be sure to click on the maximize button of the Program Manager window, not another window).
3. Click on the Window menu and click on **Cascade.** Notice the new window arrangement (see Figure 3-3).

To Tile a group of document windows,

1. Click on the Window menu and **Tile.** Notice the difference in appearance (see Figure 3-4).

When you switch from Cascade to Tile, the icons within each group window may look poorly aligned.

To arrange them neatly,

1. Make one of the windows *active* by clicking anywhere in it.

2. Click on the Window menu and Arrange Icons.
3. Repeat for the other group windows.

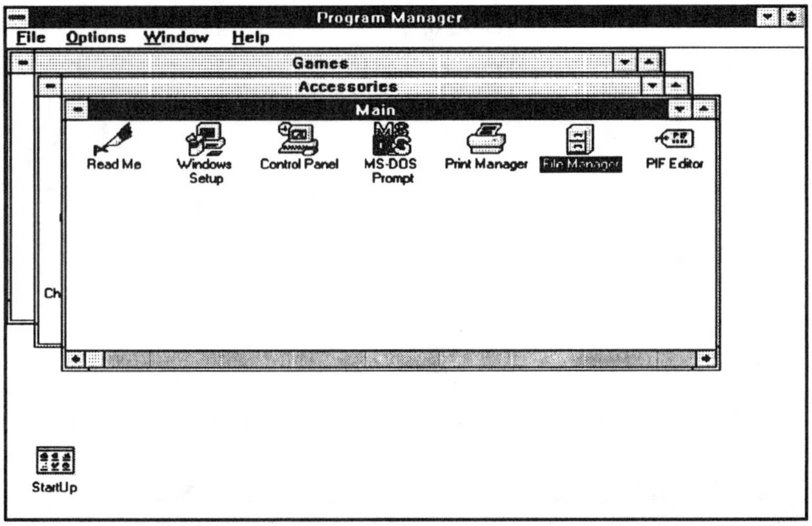

Figure 3-3: *Cascade of Group Windows*

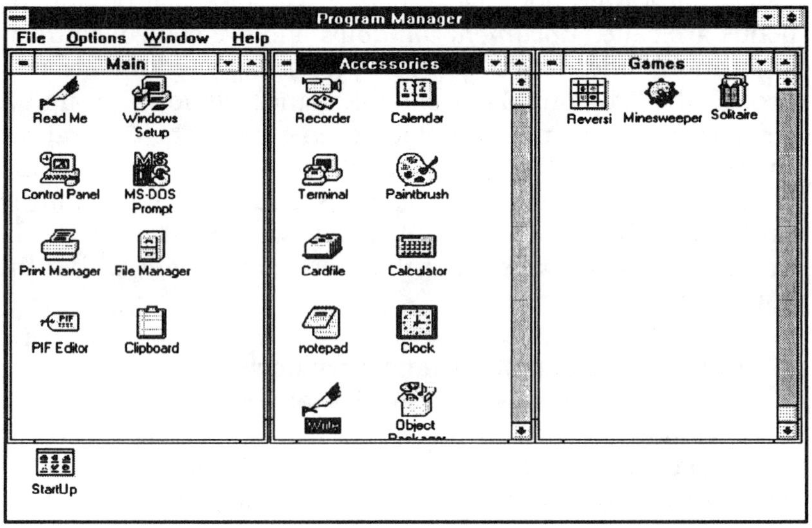

Figure 3-4: *Tiled Group Windows*

If you are tired of the Cascade or Tile arrangement, you can close each window, returning it to an icon or you can resize and move each window. There is no quick way to return the windows to the last arrangement you had before you chose Cascade or Tile.

Note: The Options menu includes Save Settings on Exit. If this is checked, when you leave Windows your settings (for example Tiled or Cascaded windows) will be saved and you will see them again when you next enter the Program Manager. If Save Settings on Exit is not checked, you will return to the default settings when you re-enter the Program Manager. To check or uncheck the option, click on it.

Using the Task List to Open More Than One Application

In Lesson 1 we learned to open and close a single application. However, one of the strengths of Windows is that you can keep many applications open simultaneously, switching from one to the other with a few clicks of the mouse.

The *Task List* provides a record of all open applications. It is actually a dialog box. This list always includes the Program Manager, since the Program Manager must be running when Windows is open. To open a second or subsequent application, first use the Task List to switch from an open application *back* to the Program Manager. Then, from the Program Manager, open the next application.

Before you begin this exercise,

1. Close the Main and Games group windows by double-clicking on the control menu box of each.
2. Leave the Accessories window open.
3. Resize the Accessories window, if necessary, so that you can see every icon.

To open more than one application,

1. From the Accessories window, double-click on the Notepad icon to open that application. Opening the Notepad may or may not hide the Accessories window.
2. Press CTRL+ESC to reach the Task list (see Figure 3-5).

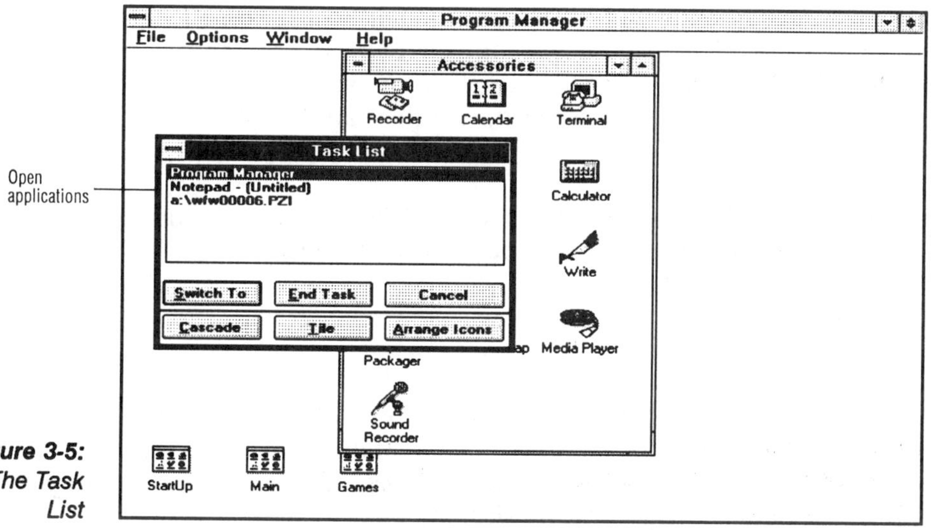

Figure 3-5: The Task List

3. At the Task List, double-click on **Program Manager.** You will return to the Accessories window. The Notepad window will probably be hidden, *but it is still open.*

4. Double-click on the Cardfile icon to open that application.
5. Press CTRL+ESC to reach the Task List and double-click on **Program Manager.**
6. Now open the application called Paintbrush.

Pressing CTRL+ESC is not the only way to reach the Task List. You may prefer to use one of the following methods.

Double-clicking to Reach the Task List

Note: This method will work only if part of the Desktop is visible. If not, use one of the other methods.

1. Click on the Restore button of the Program Manager. (It is found in the upper right corner of the Program Manager window and contains two triangles.)
2. Double-click anywhere on the Desk top (the background area of your screen).
3. At the Task List, click on Cancel.

Using **Switch To...** to Reach the Task List

1. From the Program Manager window, click on its control menu and click on
   Switch To...
2. At the Task List, click on Cancel.

You can use the control menu of any application to reach the Task List. Don't get confused, however, and click on the control menu of the Accessories window. You won't find the **Switch To...** command within a document window—only in an application window.

Once your applications are open, use the task list to switch from one to another.

To Switch from one application to another, using the Task List,

1. Open the task list if it is not already open.
2. Double-click on Notepad.
3. Return to the task list.
4. Double-click on Cardfile.

You can Cascade and Tile your application windows, but *not* from the Window menu. The Cascade and Tile commands on the Window menu will work only for document group windows. To Cascade and Tile your application windows, use the Task List.

To Cascade and Tile application windows,

1. Open the Task List.
2. Click on Cascade.

3. Open the Task List.
4. Click on Tile.

The Task List is also handy for closing an application.

To close an application from the Task List,
1. Open the task list, if it is not open already, by pressing CTRL+ESC.
2. Click on Cardfile.
3. Click on the command button marked End Task to close the Cardfile.
4. Close the Notepad and Paintbrush from the Task List.
5. The Program Manager will be reduced in size. Expand its frame and move it to the center of your screen.

The Task List has one more important use—*giving you information!* In the Windows environment, when many applications are often open but not visible, the Task List will always display every application that is running (see Figure 3-6). So when you aren't sure if an application is open, look at the Task List! This can prevent you from opening a second copy of the same application, and wasting valuable space in memory.

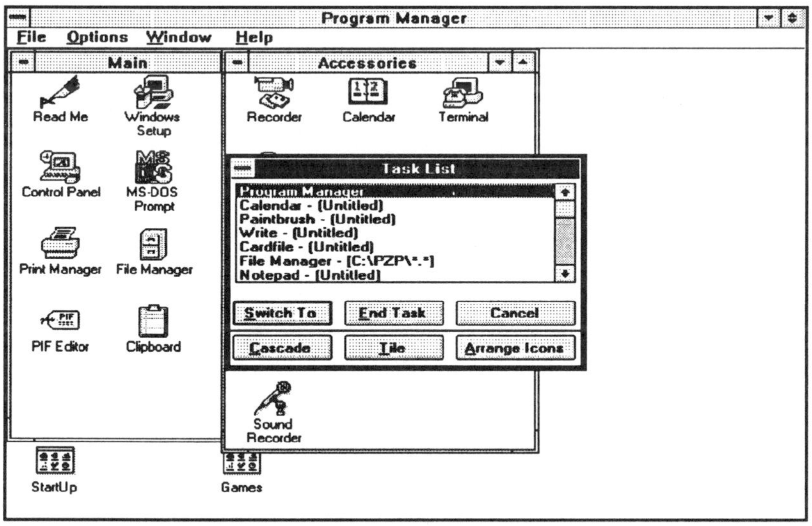

Figure 3-6: This user has many open applications

Review Exercises

1. Close all open program group windows.
2. From the Window menu open the Accessories, Main, and Games windows.
3. Tile the program group windows (they may be tiled already).
4. A. Make the Games program group active.
   B. Use the Window menu to arrange all of the icons in that group neatly.

5. A. Double-click on its icon to open the game Reversi.
   B. If Reversi is blocking access to the Games window, use the Task List to switch to the Program Manager, then open Solitaire and Minesweeper from the Games window.
6. A. Reduce Minesweeper to an icon.
   B. Switch to Solitaire. (Hint: from the Task List, double-click on Solitaire.)
7. Cascade all the applications. Notice that Minesweeper (an icon) is not included in the Cascade.
8. Use the Task List to switch to the Program Manager and open the calculator, clock and notepad—all from Accessories. (Hint: you may need to enlarge the window to see all the icons.)
9. Tile all the applications. (Hint: at the Task List, click on Tile.)
10. Close each application (except for the Program Manager) and return to the Program Manager window.
11. Resize the Program Manager so that it fills approximately two-thirds of the screen.

4

Using Windows Help

The objectives of this lesson are to

- Access the Help function
- Understand Help terminology
- Search for a topic in Help

In Windows, *every* application offers you help when you need it. Help always appears as the last item on an application's main menu.

Although you reach Help directly from your application, it is actually a separate application. Therefore, you can close the application you are in and find that Help is still running. Always remember that Help, like any other application, will stay open until you close it.

Also remember that each application has a *different* Help function. If you need Help for Windows Write, you won't get it if the active application is the Program Manager. Always be sure that you are *in* the application for which you need Help.

You can reach Help in any of these ways:

1. Click on Help from the main menu.
2. Press **F1**.
3. Click on the Help command button in a dialog box.

To use the Program Manager Help menu,

1. Make the Program Manager active. (hint: click on any part of its window)
2. Click on the word **Help** (see Figure 4-1).
3. Notice the choices on the Help menu.

Contents. An alphabetized listing of Help topics.
Search for Help on.... Lets you search for the topic of your choice.

How to Use Help. For new Windows users.
Windows Tutorial. Available only from Program Manager Help.
About.... Statistics and information about the current application.

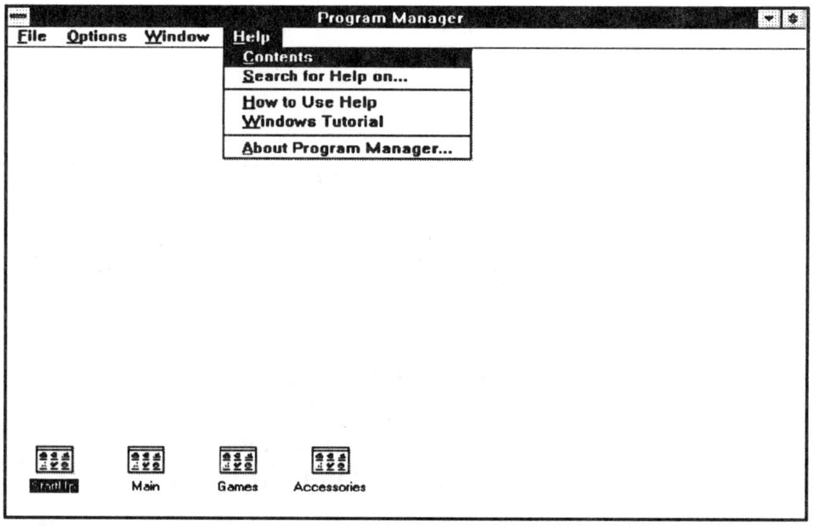

Figure 4-1: The Program Manager Help Menu

Using the Contents Menu

The contents screen contains an alphabetized list of every topic covered. We will learn how to scroll this listing so you can see the topics that are covered.

To reach the Contents screen,

1. Click on **Contents** (see Figure 4-2).

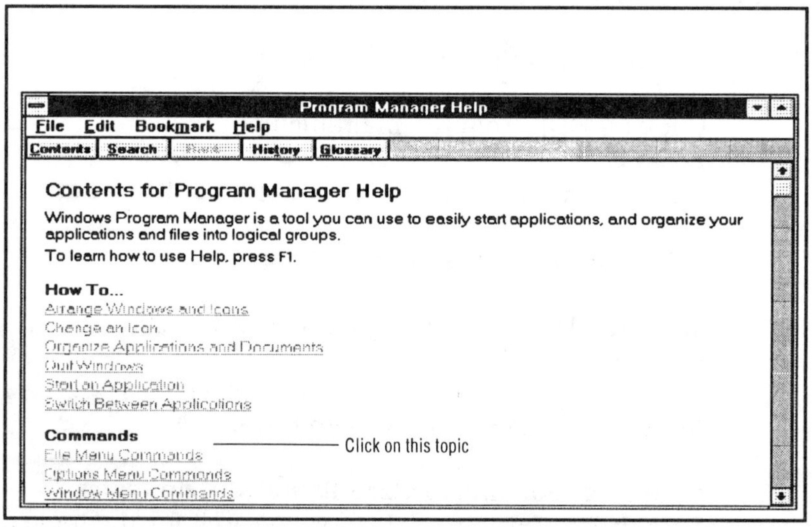

Figure 4-2: Contents Screen for Program Manager Help

If the screen is not entirely visible, you will see a vertical scroll bar at the right side of your window.

To *scroll* the Contents listing,

1. Click on the down scroll arrow at the right side of the Help screen. You can click repeatedly to scroll the screen slowly, or you can keep the mouse button down to scroll more rapidly.

Topics described in Help will be printed in green with *solid* underlines. These are called *jump terms*, because when you click on one you will jump to another screen where the topic is explained.

Note: Be sure you are still at the Contents screen for Program Manager Help.

To use a jump term,

1. Click on the topic **File Menu Commands.**

You will jump to the screen called **File Menu Commands**. This screen explains the Commands on the Program Manager File menu.
Terms explained in Help will be printed in green with *dotted* underlines. These are called *definition terms*, because when you click on one, Windows will display a definition of the term.

To use a definition term,

1. Point to the definition term: **scroll bar.**
2. Click on it.
3. Read the definition of **scroll bar.**
4. Click again to remove the definition from your screen.
5. Use the vertical scroll bar at the right of the screen to scroll the entire list of File menu commands.

Each definition term is also contained in the Help glossary. You can view the entire Glossary.

To view the Glossary,
1. Click on the button marked **Glossary**.
2. Scroll the list of definition terms.
3. Click on any term to view its definition.
4. Click again to remove the definition from your screen.
5. Close the Glossary (hint: double-click on the control menu box in the upper left corner of the glossary window).

When you aren't sure of the exact name of the topic you need Help with, use the Search feature. You can reach the Search feature from the Help menu or from the command button that appears on most Help screens.

To use Search to get Help on starting applications,

1. Click on the **Search** button (see Figure 4-3).

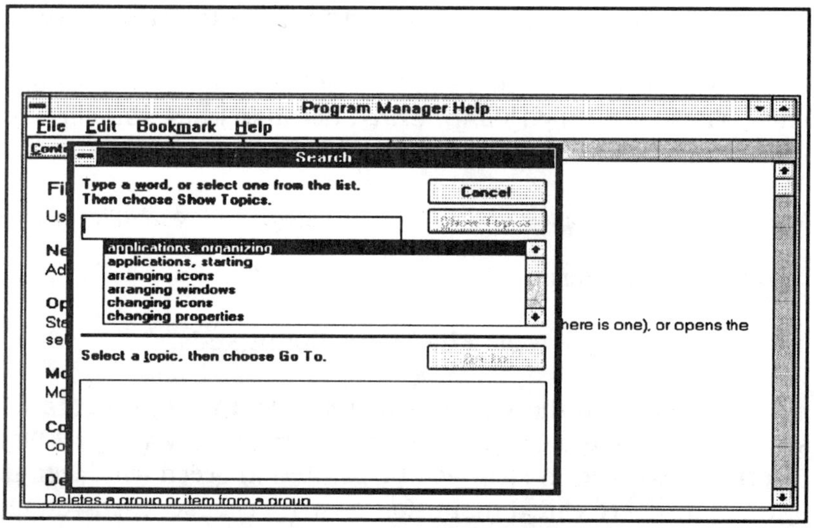

Figure 4-3: The Search Dialog Box

2. Scroll the list of topics to locate **Starting Applications.**
3. Click to select it.
4. Click on the **Show Topics** button.
5. Look at the list of topics at the *bottom* of the screen.
6. Select **Starting an Application When You Start Windows** (see Figure 4-4).
7. Choose **Go To**.

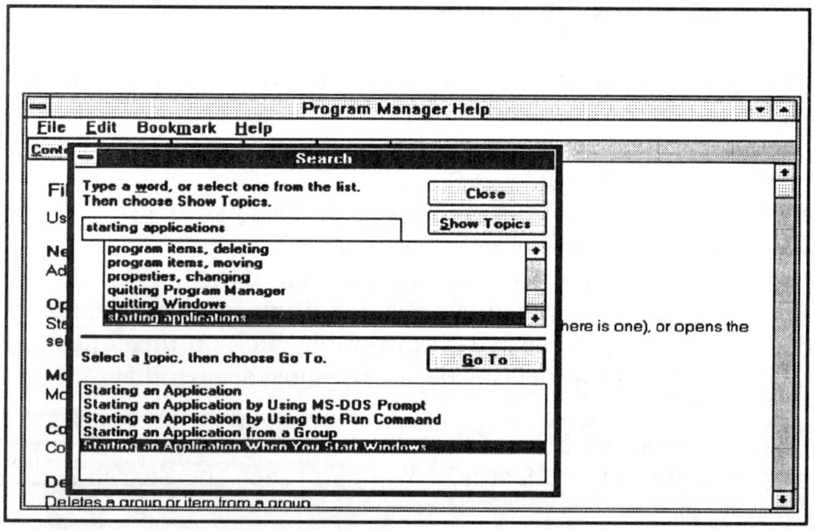

Figure 4-4: Using the Search Dialog Box

Retracing Your Steps

Two of the command buttons are helpful in reminding you of topics or screens you have used during your Help session.

1. **Back.** Takes you back to each previous *screen* you have seen in your Help session.
2. **History.** Displays a list of every *topic* you have chosen during your Help session.

Leaving Help

Remember that Help is an application and will continue to run until you Exit. You can leave Help as you would any other application. Use *one* of the following methods to exit from Help.

1. Double-click the control menu box.
2. Open the control menu and choose Close.
3. Open the File menu and choose Exit.

To exit from Help,

1. Open the File menu and choose Exit.

Review Exercises

1. Open the Program Manager Help menu.
2. Choose **About Program Manager** and learn which mode your computer is using to run Windows 3.1. Click on OK.
3. A. Choose Contents from the Help menu.
   B. Get help on Window Menu Commands.
4. Look up the meaning of the term **group icon**.
5. A. Go back to the previous screen.
   B. Get Help on Organizing Applications and Documents.
6. Get Help on moving a program item.
7. A. Use the Glossary to find the meanings of the terms **command button, desktop, title bar**.
   B. Close the Glossary.
8. Use Search to find information on creating your own icons.
9. Move back through previous screens to reach the Contents screen.
10. Close Program Manager Help.

5

Using Windows Write

The objectives of this lesson are to

- Open and Close Windows Write
- Open a file
- Insert and Delete text
- Select, Move, and Copy text
- Format a document
- Save a document
- Print a document

In this lesson, we will look at Windows Write, a word processing application which is one of the Windows Accessories. We will do so for two important reasons: first, because Write is a convenient, easy-to-use application for those who do not need a full-featured and expensive word processing program, and second, because the basic tasks you will learn to do in Windows Write *can be done the same way in every Windows application*. Once you learn to open a file, save a file, print, select, move, and copy text, you will know how to handle these tasks throughout the Windows environment.

Note: Make sure your Student Data disk is inserted into the correct drive for this entire lesson.

To open **Windows Write,**

1. Return to the Program Manager, if you are not there already.
2. Open the Accessories program group window.
3. If the window is not big enough to display the Write icon, either enlarge the frame by dragging it, or scroll the window until the **Write** icon is visible.
4. Double-click the **Write** icon.

As you look at the Write screen (see Figure 5-1), you will notice that most of the elements are already familiar to you. There are three additional elements you need to understand:

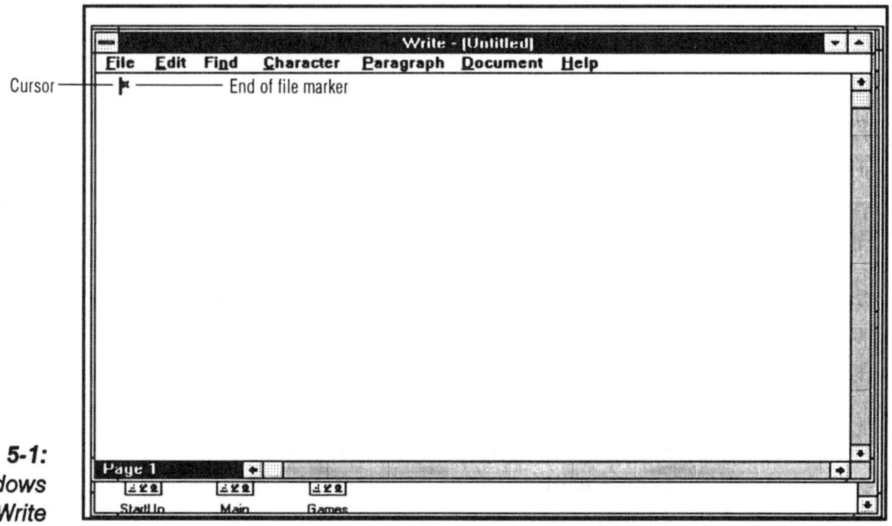

Figure 5-1: *Windows Write*

1. **Insertion Point.** Usually called a cursor. Appears as a blinking, vertical line. Shows you where the next typed character will appear.
2. **End Mark.** Indicates the end of the document. Appears directly after the insertion point in a new document. When you type, your text will appear *between* the insertion point and the end mark.
3. **Mouse Pointer.** Appears as a slender I in any area where you can type, and a single-headed arrow elsewhere on the screen.

We will open a file created in Windows Write that has been saved on your Student Data disk.

To open a file,

1. At the menu, click on **File.**
2. Click on **Open**.
3. At the **Open** dialog box (see Figure 5-2) look at the area marked **Drives**. If the drive listed is *not* the one containing your Student Data disk, open the list box by clicking on the down arrow to the right.
4. Click on the correct drive. If you need to scroll the list box, there will be a vertical scroll bar for you to use.
   When you have selected the correct drive, the list of files in the **File Name** area of the dialog box will contain the files on your Student Data disk.

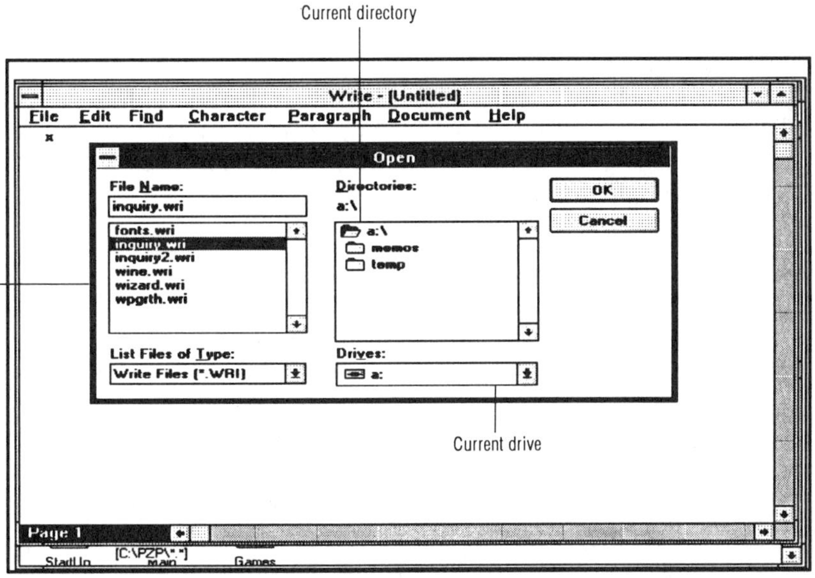

Figure 5-2: The Open Dialog Box

5. Click on the filename **inquiry.wri** and then click on OK (if you prefer, you may double-click on the filename).
6. If necessary, maximize or enlarge the Write window.

Moving Around the Document

Now that we have an open document (see Figure 5-3), we are going to make some editing changes. In order to do so, we need to move efficiently around the document. The quickest way to move your cursor (insertion point) is with the mouse.

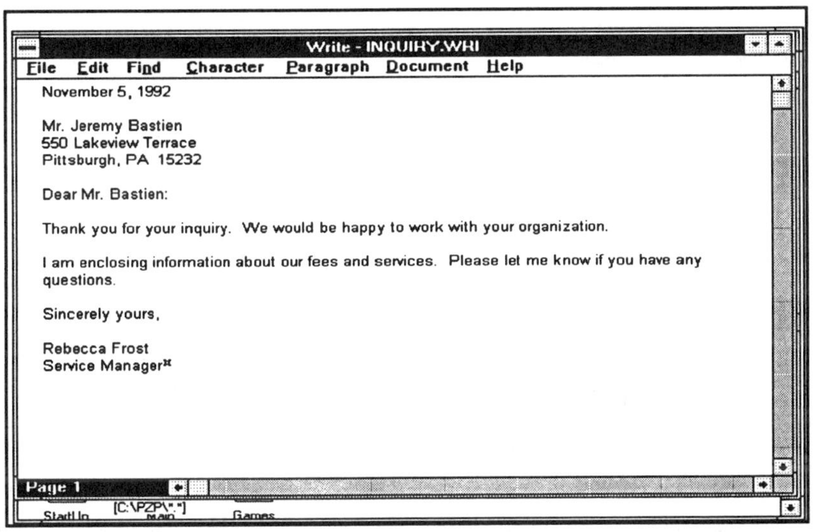

Figure 5-3: INQUIRY

To move your cursor with the mouse,

1. Point to the place in the document where you want the cursor to appear.
2. Click.

There are also several shortcut key combinations you may want to use for moving your cursor. The following shortcuts will work with *all* Windows applications.

KEYS	CURSOR MOVES TO
RIGHT OR LEFT ARROW	Next character to the left or right
UP OR DOWN ARROW	Next line up or down
CTRL + RIGHT ARROW	Next word to the right
CTRL + LEFT ARROW	Next word to the left
HOME	Left end of the current line
END	Right end of the current line
CTRL + HOME	Beginning of the document
CTRL + END	End of the document

Table 5-1: *Shortcut Key Combinations*

Wordwrap

Like almost all word processors, Windows Write automatically wraps and rewraps your lines as you enter and edit your text. Let the word-wrap feature do its job—do not press ENTER to reach the next line, unless your text does not reach the right margin.

Inserting and Deleting Text

The ability to insert additional text anywhere within a document and delete unwanted material is one of the simplest, yet most powerful jobs of a word processor.

To insert text,

1. Move the mouse pointer just before the word **to** in the first paragraph of **INQUIRY** and click.
2. Add the words **to have the opportunity.**
3. Move the mouse pointer just before the second sentence in paragraph two and click.
4. Add the sentence: **Mary Ann Barnett, one of our sales associates, will be calling you to see if you have any questions.** Notice that Wordwrap has automatically moved the second sentence down (see Figure 5-4).

If you notice yourself make a mistake as you type, you can delete the error by using the BACKSPACE key. For other deletions, use the Delete key.

To delete text,

1. Your cursor should be positioned just before the closing sentence of paragraph two. If not, move it there and click.
2. Press the Delete key repeatedly until the entire sentence has been removed.

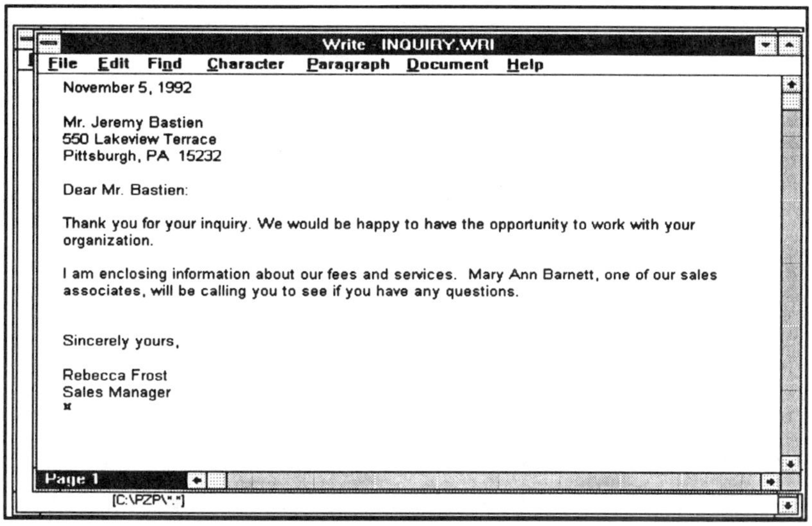

Figure 5-4: *The document INQUIRY with changes*

Inserting and Deleting Lines

As you edit your Write document, you will need to add or remove lines. It is impossible to predict exactly when this will occur—but you will typically have to add or remove lines when you have inserted or deleted text, or when you have copied or moved text.

Use the following instructions to add or remove blank lines.

To delete a blank line,

1. Position your cursor on the blank line and press **DELETE**.

To insert a blank line,

1. Position your cursor on either:
   the end of the preceding line, or
   the beginning of the next line
2. Press **ENTER**.

To bring text from one line up to the line above,

1. Position your cursor at the location where you want to move text.
2. Press **DELETE** to move the text up to the cursor.

Selecting Text

In order to change text that is onscreen, you must first select it. Selecting highlights a block of text. This text will be altered by the next command. To select text, first move your mouse pointer to the beginning of the text to be selected. Then, click, and holding the mouse button down, drag the mouse over the text. Drag to the *right* to select one character at a time. Drag *down* to select one line at a time. Be sure that the text you have selected is highlighted. To remove the selection, click on any part of the screen.

To select text,

1. Position the cursor at the beginning of the line containing the date.
2. Drag the mouse across the line and release the mouse button.

To remove the selection,

1. Click on any part of the screen.

Shortcuts for Selecting Text

You can select text with your mouse pointer in two different shapes.

1. When your mouse pointer is on any part of the screen where you can type, it resembles the letter **I**.
2. When you move your mouse pointer into the left margin area, it changes to a single-headed arrow.

Here are several shortcuts you can use to select text:

Mouse Shape	To Select	Method
I	Sentence	Point anywhere within the sentence. Hold down the CTRL key and click.
I	Word	Point anywhere in the word and double-click.
Arrow	Line	Point to the line and click.
Arrow	Entire Document	Point to any line in the document. Hold down the CTRL key and click.

Table 5-2: *Shortcuts for Selecting Text*

To select text using mouse shortcuts,

1. Move the mouse pointer into the left margin (arrow shape).
2. Point to the line that reads: **Dear Mr. Bastien** and click. This shortcut selects the entire line.
3. Remove the selection by clicking anywhere onscreen.
4. Position your cursor anywhere within the word **Pittsburgh** and double-click. This selects the entire word.
5. Remove the selection.
6. Point to the document from the left margin, press the CTRL key, and click. This shortcut selects the entire document.
7. Remove the selection.
8. Position your cursor anywhere within the sentence that begins **I am enclosing information**, hold down the CTRL key, and click. This will select the entire sentence.
9. Remove the selection.

Moving and Copying Text

Now that you can select text you will be able to move and copy parts of your document. Moving and copying involve the use of the Windows Clipboard, an area of memory used by all Windows applications to hold text and pictures during a move or copy procedure.

Note: Remember that moving removes text from its current location and places it in a new location whereas copying duplicates the text so it appears in two different locations.

To move text,

1. Select the entire sentence that begins: **We would be happy** (hint: Position your cursor anywhere within the sentence, hold down the CTRL key and click).
2. From the menu, choose **Edit.**
3. From the menu, choose **Cut**.
4. Move your mouse pointer just past the last sentence of the document and click.
5. From the menu, choose **Edit** and **Paste** (see Figure 5-5).

To copy text,

1. Select the line containing the date.
2. From the menu, choose **Edit** and **Copy**.
3. Move the cursor to the next blank line.
4. From the menu, choose **Paste** (see Figure 5-6).

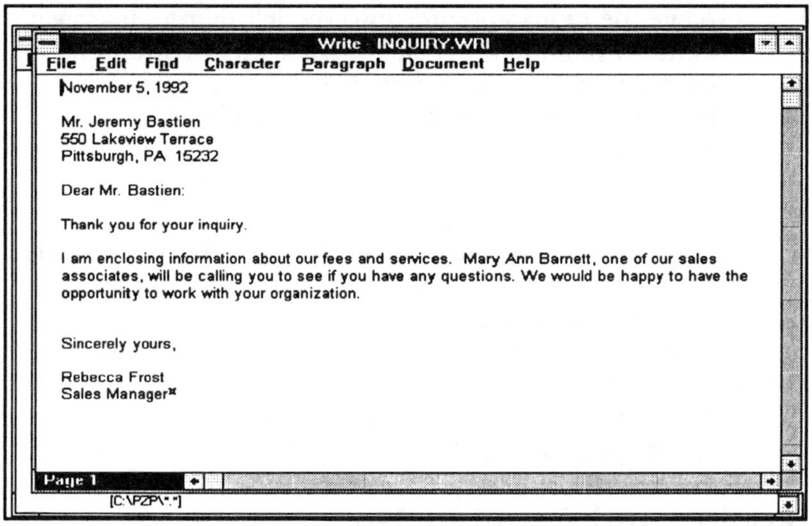

Figure 5-5: *INQUIRY, updated*

Duplicate date

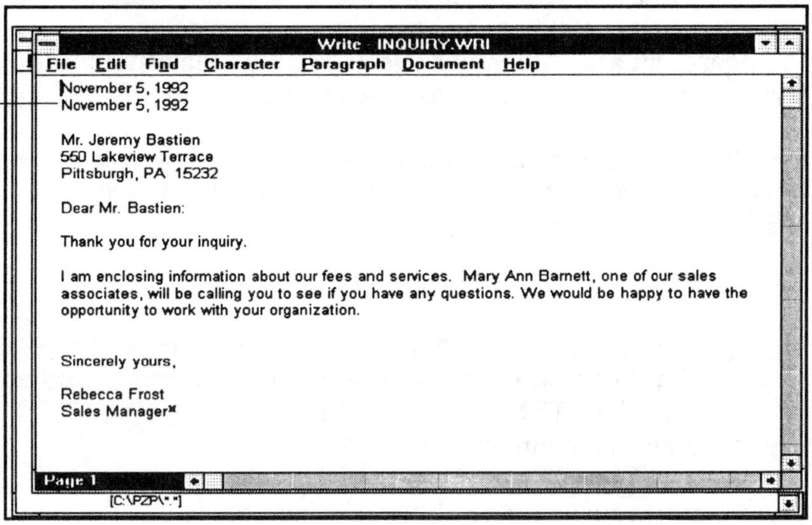

Figure 5-6: *INQUIRY, with date copied*

We have learned to delete, one character at a time, by repeatedly pressing the **Delete** key. Once you know how to select text, you can delete an entire block of text.

To delete an block of text,

1. Select the copy of the date you made in the previous exercise.
2. Press **Delete**.

Note: Remember that after these procedures you may need to add or delete lines. To do so, follow the directions given earlier in this lesson.

Formatting Your Document

Formatting changes the *appearance* of your document, not the meaning. In **Write,** there are three menus that contain formatting commands.

1. **Character.** These commands affect the appearance of the characters, and include font size and style, bold, italic, and underline.
2. **Paragraph.** These commands affect an entire paragraph (or more) and include alignment, line spacing, and indents.
3. **Document.** These commands affect the document as a whole and include margins, tabs, headers, and footers.

Character Formatting

Before you can format text that is onscreen, you must select it. After text is selected, choose a format from the Format Character menu. We will add the italics format to parts of our letter. Once you can do this, you can add other character formats in the same way.

To italicize text already typed,

1. Select the words: **Sales Manager**
2. From the menu, choose **Character** and **Italic.**
3. Remove the selection highlight by clicking anywhere onscreen.
4. To return to normal type, choose **Character** and **Regular**.

The procedure is slightly different when you are formatting as you create text.

To italicize text as you type,

1. Move your cursor directly below Sales Manager.
2. From the menu, choose **Character** and **Italic.**
3. Type the line: **Eastern Division** (see Figure 5-7).
4. To return to normal type, choose **Character** and **Regular**.

Use the same procedures for all character formats, substituting the format of your choice for **Italic**.

Paragraph Formatting

In Write, a paragraph is defined as a portion of text of *any length* that ends with a press of the ENTER key. This means that a paragraph may be anywhere from one word to many lines long.

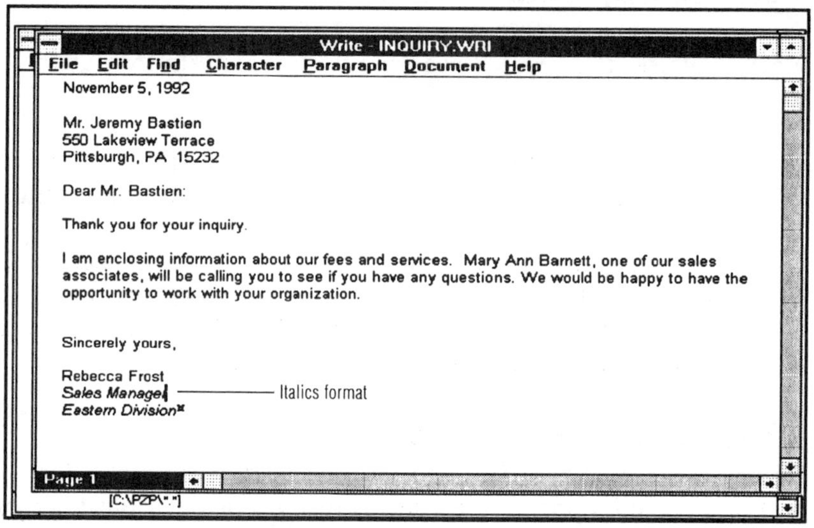

Figure 5-7: *INQUIRY, with character formats*

In Write, you can line up your paragraphs at either the left or right margin, at *both* left and right margins (called *Justified*), or centered on the page. Write considers the left alignment the "normal" or default alignment. We will learn to change alignments in our letter.

To center a paragraph,

1. Position your cursor anywhere in the first line of your document (the date). It is not necessary to select the date.
2. From the menu, choose **Paragraph** and **Centered** (See Figure 5-8).

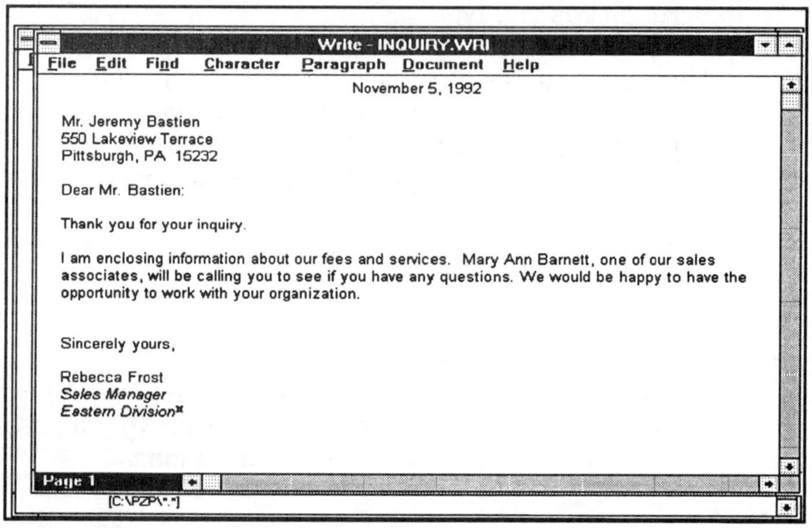

Figure 5-8: *INQUIRY, with date centered*

To right align a paragraph,

1. Position your cursor anywhere in the date.
2. From the menu, choose **Paragraph** and **Right**.

To return to left alignment.

1. Position your cursor anywhere in the date.
2. From the menu, choose **Paragraph** and **Normal**.

Document Formatting

Document formatting is used to choose formats that will affect the entire document. We will learn to change the margins for your letter.

To change margins,

1. From the menu, choose **Document** and **Page Layout** (see Figure 5-9).

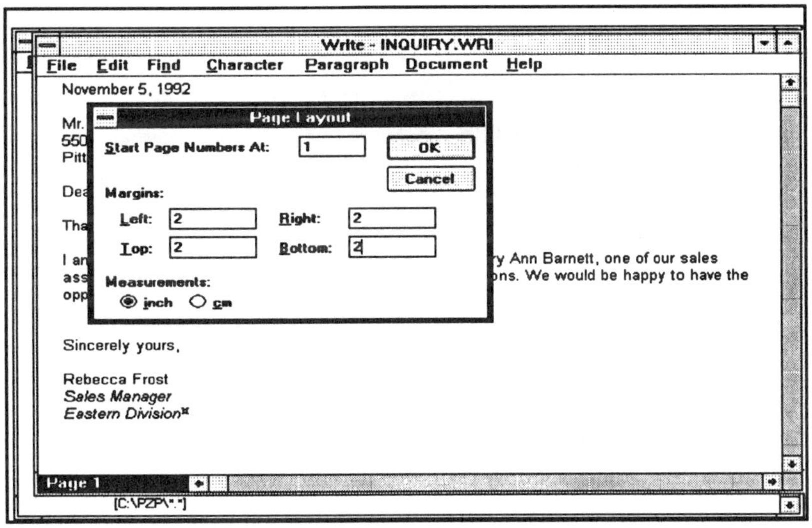

Figure 5-9: *The Page Layout Dialog Box*

2. Press the TAB key until the left margin box is selected.
3. Type a **2** to change the left margin to 2 inches.
4. TAB to the right margin box and type a **2**.
5. TAB to the top and bottom margin boxes and change them to 2 inches also.
6. Click on OK. You can't see the actual margins until you print your document, but you can see that there are fewer words in each line of the paragraph.

Note: By choosing Document and Ruler On you can display the Write ruler. You can use the ruler to set margins, tabs, alignment, and line spacing. Any changes made at the ruler will be reflected in the corresponding dialog box.

Saving a File

It is a good idea to save your work frequently. There are two Save commands on the file menu, **Save** and **Save As...** They are used as follows:

1. **Save As...** Used to save a file for the *first* time. You are required to give the file a name. Also used to resave a file using a *different* name. The current file and the original file *both* remain on your disk.
2. **Save.** Used to re-save a file using the same name. The current file replaces the original file. You do *not* give the file a name with this procedure.

Your letter was saved with the filename **INQUIRY**. We will save it under a different name, **INQUIRY2**.

To save a file using a different name,

1. From the menu, choose **File** and **Save As...** (see Figure 5-10).

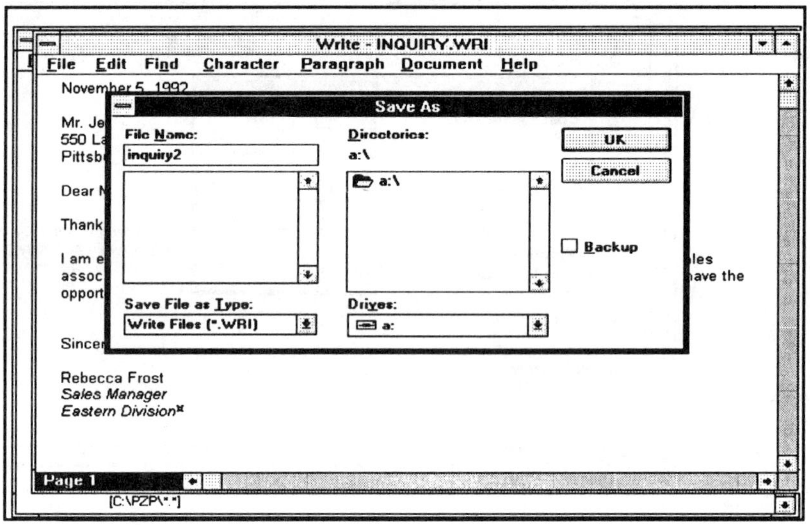

Figure 5-10: *The Save As Dialog Box*

2. At the **Save As** dialog box, check to see which drive is current. If the drive listed is *not* the one on which you want to save your letter, change the drive to the one containing your Student Data disk (instructions can be found earlier in this lesson).
3. The words in the **File Name** text box will probably be selected. If *not*, move your cursor there by clicking on the box.
4. Type the new name for your letter, **INQUIRY2**. Do not include a file extension, because Write automatically includes the extension **.WRI** on all documents. Delete any extra text in the box.
5. Click on OK.

Printing a Document

Now that your letter has been saved with its editing changes, you are ready to print. Because printing involves sending your document to another device, there are a number of things that can go wrong. Therefore, *always save your document before you print.*
By doing so, you can avoid the frustration of dealing with printer problems and lost data.

To print a document,

1. From the menu, choose **File** and **Print**.
2. Make sure the printer listed at the top of the dialog box is the one you are printing to. If not, click on **Setup**. and change to a different printer in the Setup dialog box. When you have completed your work in the Setup box, click on OK to return to the Print dialog box.
3. At the Print dialog box, click on OK.

Beginning a New Document

Our work on our letter is done, and we are ready to begin work on a new document. Beginning a new document will bring up a fresh screen, clearing the present document.

To begin a new document,

1. From the menu, choose **File** and **New.**
   If you have made changes since the last time you saved your document, Write will ask if you want those changes to be saved. Once you have clicked on **Yes** or **No**, you will see a new document screen.
2. Type your name and address on the first three lines of the new document screen.

Using Windows 3.1 True Type Fonts

An important new feature of Windows 3.1, True Type Fonts offer you four styles of fonts in scalable sizes. These fonts are available to everyone who uses Windows 3.1, regardless of which brand or style of printer you use.

The advantage of scalable fonts is that they can be used in a wide range of sizes; indeed, these fonts are available in any point size (whole numbers only) between 4 and 127 points (72 points = 1 inch). Moreover, True Type fonts can be printed by all printers that support Windows. Now, no matter how modest a printer you have, you have at your command a great variety of styles and sizes of type.

To change fonts,

1. Select your name and address (see Figure 5-11).

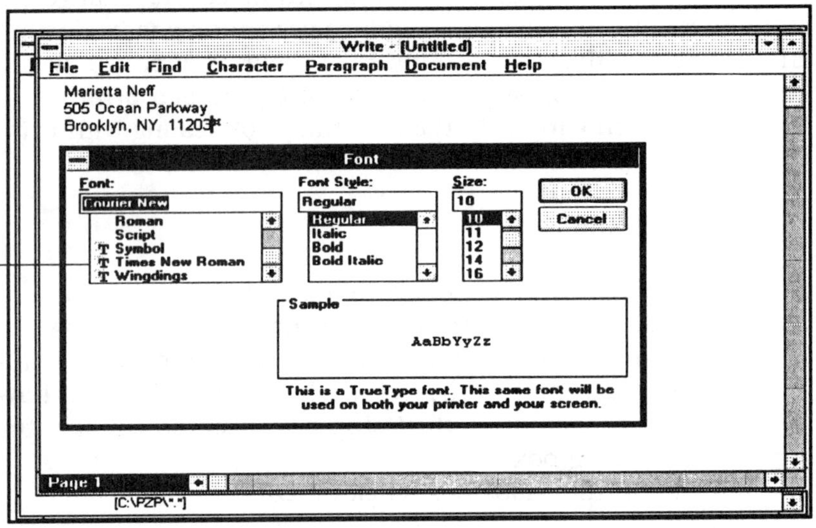

Figure 5-11: *The Font Dialog Box*

2. From the menu, choose **Character** and **Fonts**.
3. The current font will be selected.
4. Scroll the list of fonts. True Type fonts will be preceded by the letters TT. Other fonts listed are available for your current printer, but not necessarily for other printers you may use.
5. Select **Times New Roman** from your list and click on OK.
6. Remove the selection highlight by clicking anywhere onscreen, and notice the change in your document.

To change the size of your font,

1. Select the same text and choose **Character** and **Fonts.**
2. Scroll the list of sizes and choose another **Size**. Click on OK.
3. Remove the selection and notice the change in your document.

To change the style of your font,

1. Select the same text and choose **Character** and **Fonts.**
2. Change the style by clicking on either **Bold**, **Italic,** or **Bold Italic**.
3. Click on OK.

Conclusion

In this lesson, we have covered the necessary commands for using Windows Write. As you continue to use this application you will discover and use many more commands and options than we have been able to explore.

To End Your Write Session,

1. Save the current document, calling it **FONTS** (hint: choose File and Save As).
2. Exit from Write (hint: use either File Exit or the control menu).

Review Exercises

1. Open Windows Write.
2. Open the file called: **WIZARD**
3. Add the following sentence to the end of paragraph 2:
   Auditions have been tentatively scheduled for the last week in May.
4. Delete the sentence in paragraph 3 that begins: **We need to know**
5. In paragraph 3, change the word **kids** to **children** (hint: delete **kids** and insert **children**).
6. Underline the names **The Wizard of Oz** and **Peter Pan**.
7. Insert 3 additional blank lines between **Sincerely yours,** and **Jerry Wynne**.
8. Add the following sentence to the end of paragraph 1:
   We all enjoyed working with you last year.
9. Move the sentence you just added to the beginning of paragraph 2.
10. Delete the words **last summer** from the sentence that begins: **People are still talking**
11. Change the top and bottom margins to 2".
12. Change the left and right margins to 1.5".
13. Save the document as **WIZARD2**.
14. Print the document.
15. Exit from Windows Write.

6
Exploring Windows Accessories

The objectives of this lesson are to introduce the following Windows accessories:

- Clock
- Cardfile
- Calendar
- Notepad

Now that you are able to use Windows Write, learning to use the remaining Windows accessories will be much easier. These simple-to-use programs are designed to make your daily task routines faster and more efficient. Many are electronic versions of the usual conveniences found on every desktop. Although each accessory fills a different need, the basic techniques for interacting with Windows remain the same.

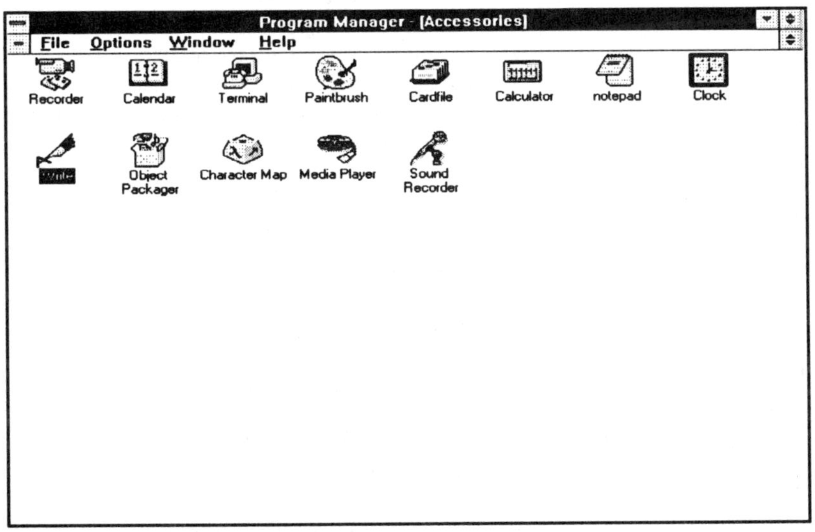

Figure 6-1: *Windows 3.1 Accessories*

This lesson will introduce you to several of the accessories (see Figure 6-1). For complete information about each, refer to the Windows documentation. The following table describes important features of the Windows 3.1 accessories.

Accessory	Functions
Calculator	• Can function in standard or scientific mode. • In standard mode performs simple calculations, percentages, square roots. • In scientific mode performs simple scientific and statistical calculations. • In scientific mode can work in binary, octal, and hexadecimal number systems. • In statistical mode can calculate sum, sum of squares, mean, and standard deviation.
Calendar	• Can display either a Day view or Month view. • In Day view, allows you to enter and display appointments for a particular day at time intervals you choose. • Provides a scratch pad for six notes and reminders. • In Month view, shows the entire month, but not appointments. • Allows you to set an alarm for a day and time of your choice as a reminder. • Allows you to mark a calendar day with a symbol to denote a particular meaning.
Cardfile	• Can create one or more files of individual "cards," which are automatically alphabetized by the first word on the index line. • Card may be viewed individually or as a list. • Can look for a particular card by searching the information on the index line, or by scanning the entire contents of every card. • Can move or copy text. • Can insert a drawing on a card. • Can edit, add, delete, or duplicate cards. • If you have a modem, you can automatically dial a phone number from a card.
Character Map	• Can insert special characters not on the keyboard into documents created in Windows applications. • Can select a font for use in Windows applications.
Clock	• Can display the time in analog or digital format. • Will still display time when it is sized as an icon. • Can be displayed on top of other windows. • Can display seconds and/or date.
Media Player	• Can play multimedia files and control multimedia hardware devices (you must have sound card and driver installed). • Can play MIDI sounds and compact discs.

Notepad	• Provides a simple environment in which you can take notes, jot down ideas, etc. • Can word wrap (optional). • Can search for text. • Can copy/move text to other applications. • Can create a time-log document.
Object Packager	• Can link objects between applications that support linking by embedding an icon representing the object. • Part or an entire document can be packaged and linked. • Can customize the object icon.
Paintbrush	• Can create color drawings. • Can size the drawing for display. • Offers a selection of drawing tools for different effects in creating pictures and text. • Can select an area of the drawing, called a *cutout*, and work with that separately. • Can create custom colors. • Can print an entire or part of a drawing.
Recorder	• Can create simple and complex *macros* (series of recorded keystrokes). • Can play back a macro. • Can assign shortcut keys to macros. • Can change the properties of a macro.
Sound Recorder	• Can record, edit, and play sound files (you must have sound card and driver installed). • Can link sound files to other applications that accept them. • Can change the volume, speed, and echo of a sound. • Can reverse a sound.
Terminal	• If you have a modem, can connect your computer to other computers by using existing telephone lines. • Can time sessions. • Can transfer text and binary files over the telephone.

Table 6-1: *Windows 3.1 Accessories*

Note: Before you begin to work, insert your Student Data disk into the correct drive. Start Windows and open the Accessories group window. If necessary, enlarge the window so that you can see all the icons.

Using the Windows Clock

The Windows Clock displays in either analog or digital mode. One of its nicest features is that when it is minimized, the current time is still visible. In addition to controlling the clock settings, you can choose to have the clock always displayed *on top* of other applications.

To open the clock,

1. Double-click on the Clock icon in the Accessories window. If your clock appears as an icon at the bottom of the screen, double-click on that icon.

When the clock opens, it will display in either analog mode (hands) or digital mode (see Figure 6-2). If your clock shows no title bar or control buttons, double-click anywhere within the clock window to display them. The clock window can be sized and moved like any other window.

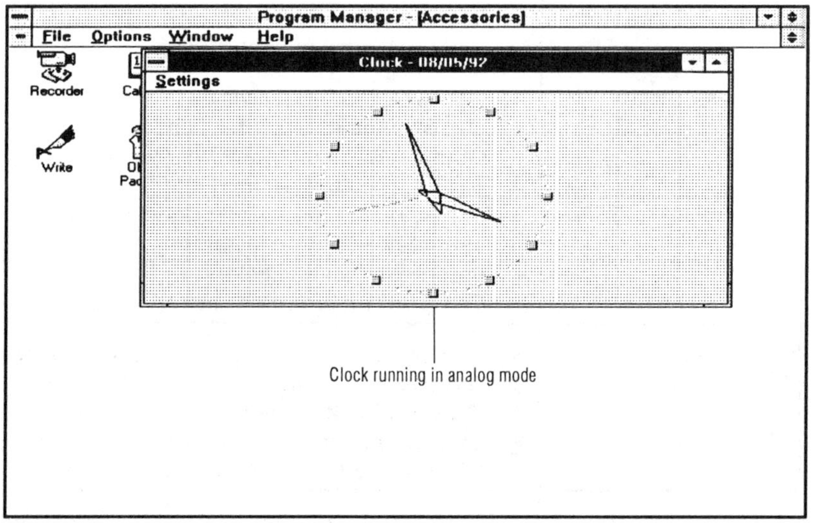

Figure 6-2: *Windows Clock*

To change from analog to digital display,

1. Open the Settings menu and click on Digital.

To minimize the clock,

1. Click on the minimize button (▾) on the Clock title bar.
   Be sure you choose the minimize button of the Clock, not the Program Manager.

Unless the Program Manager or Accessories window has been maximized, the clock icon will be visible and usable, since the current time is still displayed.

If having the current time visible is important, you can set the clock to remain on top of other open windows.

To set the clock on top of other windows,

1. Double-click on the clock icon to restore it.
2. Click on the control menu box of the clock.
3. Click on **Always on Top** to check this command.

If you want to remove this setting, repeat the procedure so that the check is removed.

4. Minimize the clock. Although not required, it is a good idea, since a clock window that remains on top will hide data in other windows.

To close the clock,

1. Close the clock as you would any other application (hint: double-click its control menu box, or, if you prefer, click once to open the control menu and click on Close).

Using the Windows Calendar

The calendar offers a daily and monthly view of your appointments. When you open it for the first time you will see a list of time intervals for the current date. When you have entered your appointments, you must be sure to *save your calendar file* so that you can open it and add to it at your next session. All Windows calendar files have the extension **.CAL**.

To open the calendar,

1. Double-click on the calendar icon in the Accessories window. Notice the date (see Figure 6-3).

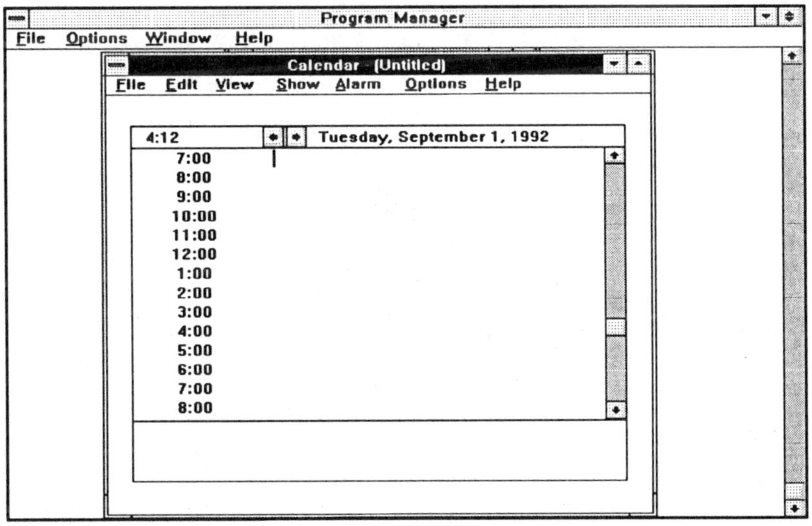

Figure 6-3: *Windows Calendar*

To move to a date in the future,

1. Click three times on the right arrow next to the date to move ahead three days.

To move to a date in the past,

1. Click three times on the left arrow next to the date to move back to the present date.

To enter an appointment,

1. Click next to **10:00** to position your cursor there.
2. Type in the following information:
   Dentist appointment
3. Click next to **2:00** to move your cursor there. Type the following:
   Job Interview, Lasker Associates, 55 W. 10th Street. Suite 40D

Notice that although you can enter all your information on one line, you cannot view it at once. To scroll the text, use your left and right arrows.

The month view will *not* display specific appointments you may have entered on the daily calendar. It shows a calendar for one month with the current date highlighted. You can move forward and backward one month at a time by clicking on the left and right arrows.

To see a month view,

1. Choose View and Month from the menu (see Figure 6-4).

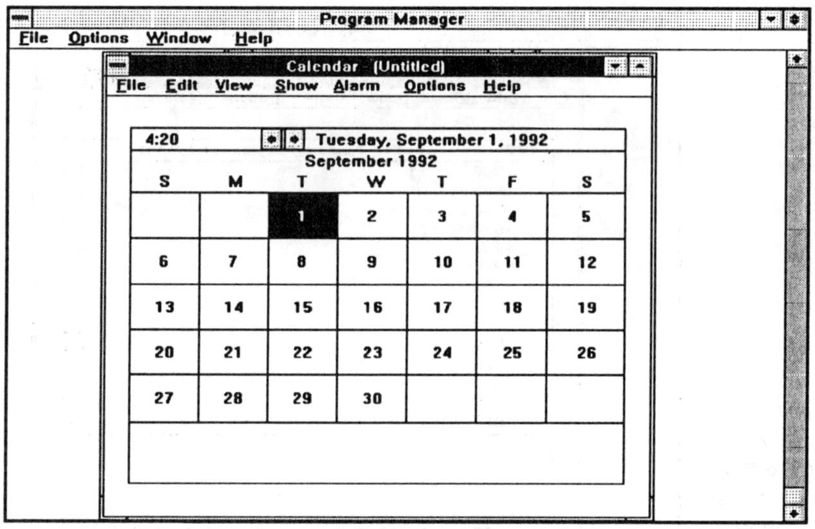

Figure 6-4: *Calendar, Month View*

2. To switch back to the daily calendar, choose View and Day.

Saving Your Calendar File

Windows allows you to keep as many different calendars as you wish. Each calendar must be saved in a separate file. Save a Windows calendar as you would any other file.

To save your calendar and close it,

1. Enter your appointments.
2. Choose File Save As.
3. If necessary, change the drive so that the calendar files are saved on your Student Data disk.
4. Type the name: **MYCAL** for your calendar. Calendar files must be named according to the rules you learned in Lesson 5 (hint: up to 8 characters, no spaces allowed). Windows will add the extension **.CAL**.
5. Click on OK or press ENTER.
6. Close the calendar, using one of the methods for closing an application.

Using the Windows Cardfile

The Windows cardfile can replace your personal telephone directory, but this is not its only use. You can create a cardfile for any set of information you would keep on index cards (recipes, bibliographic references, etc.). Windows will allow you to keep as many cardfiles as you wish. Each cardfile must be saved separately, and Windows saves each with the extension **.CRD**.

To open the Windows cardfile application,

1. Double-click on the cardfile icon in the Accessories window.

You will see a blank index card. The card has two areas, the index line and the larger data area. The cursor will be in the larger area (see Figure 6-5).

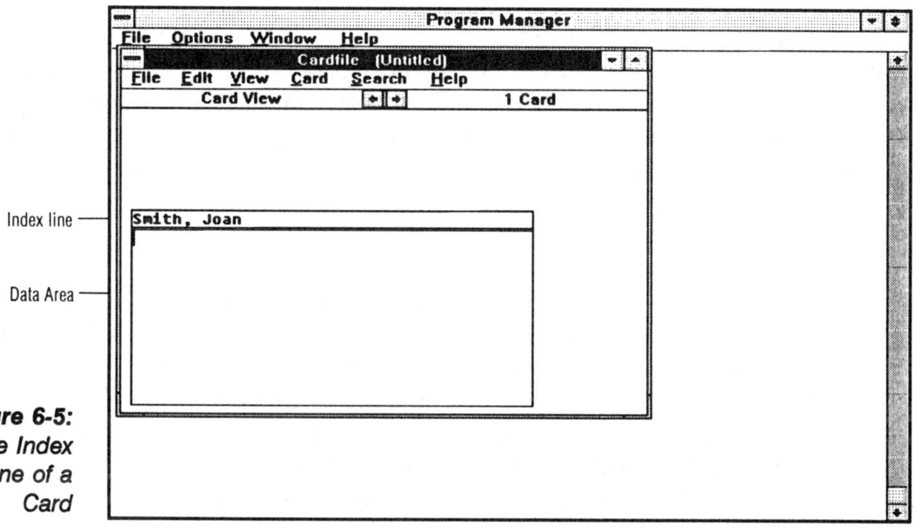

Figure 6-5: *The Index Line of a Card*

To place a name on the index line,

1. Choose Edit and Index from the menu.
2. Type your name on the index line, last name first. You can fit up to 39 characters on the index line.
3. Click on OK or press ENTER.

To enter text on the card,

1. Type an address, telephone number, or any other text, as you want it to appear on the card. Each line of your card can hold up to 40 characters.
2. When the card is full (usually 11 lines), Windows will not allow you to add any more text.

To add another card,

1. Choose Card and Add from the menu.
2. Type another name on the index line, press ENTER, and then type the text of the card.
3. Add a third card. Notice that the three cards are automatically placed in alphabetical order.

To save your cardfile,

1. Choose File Save As.
2. If necessary, correct the drive listed to save the file on your Student Data disk.
3. Type: **CARDS** as the name for your cardfile. You are allowed to use up to 8 characters, no spaces. Windows will add the extension: **CRD**.
4. Click on OK or press ENTER.

Once you have accumulated more than a few cards, finding the one you need can take time. There are several procedures that can make this task more efficient. Windows offers you commands for scrolling your cardfile, one card at a time, forward or backward, for viewing your cards as a list, and for searching for a name or other text on your card.

To scroll your cards,

1. Open the file on your Student Data disk called **MYCARD** (hint: you may need to change the drive listed in the Open dialog box).
2. Press **Page Down** several times, to scroll your cards forward. Notice that the cards are in alphabetical order.
3. Press **Page Up** several times, to scroll your cards backward.
4. Press **CTRL+End**, to bring the last card to view.
5. Press **CTRL+Home**, to bring the first card to view.

To switch to List View,

1. Choose View and List.

When you are in List View you can use your **down arrow** to scroll forward and your **up arrow** to scroll backward.

To switch to Card View,

1. Choose View and Card (see Figure 6-6).

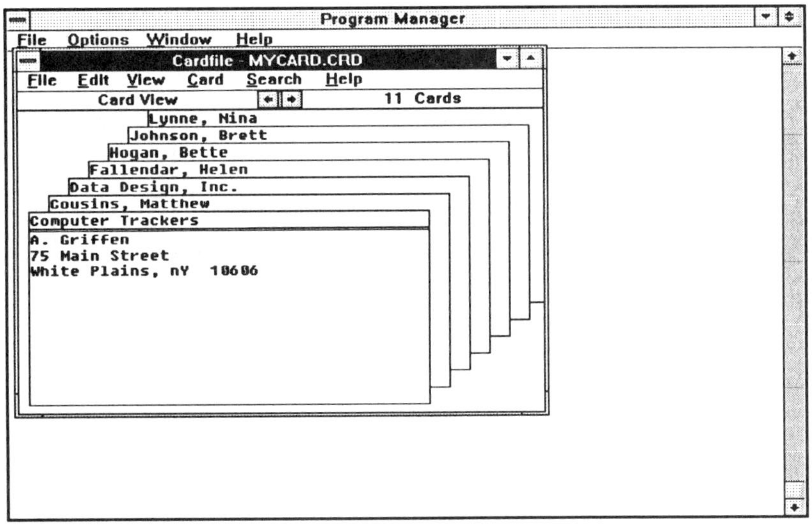

Figure 6-6: Card View

To search the Index lines of your cards,

1. Choose Search and Go To...
2. Type: **Jon**.
3. Click on OK or press ENTER.

Jonathan Peterson's card will be found.

To search the data area of your cards,

1. Choose Search and Find...
2. Type: **NY** and press ENTER (see Figure 6-7).
3. Move the Find dialog box away from your cardfile so the cards are not blocked (this may or may not be necessary).

Windows will search the main body of each card, beginning with the one currently in front. The first card found containing **NY** will be selected. To find other matches, press ENTER or choose **Find Next**. When the end of the cardfile has been reached, Windows will search from the beginning, as long as you keep pressing ENTER.

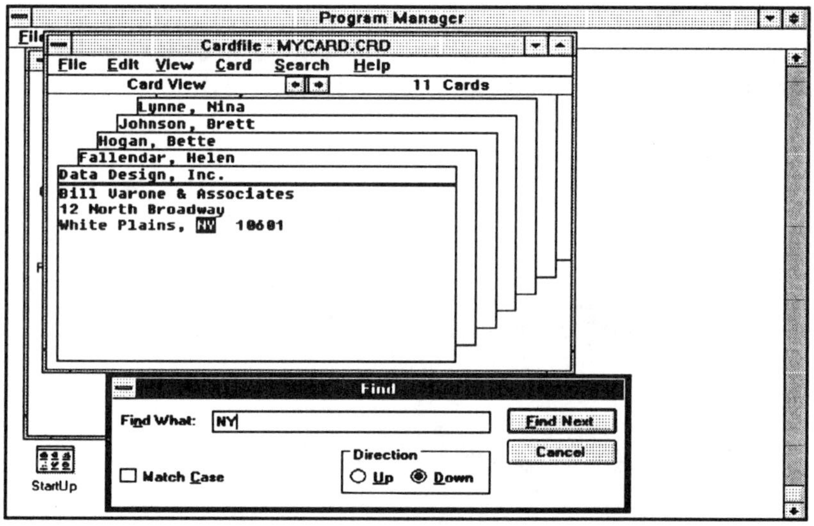

Figure 6-7: Searching the Cardfile

To Resave your cardfile, using the same name,

1. Choose File and Save.

To close the cardfile,

1. Choose File and Exit.

Using the Windows Notepad

Instead of taking notes and telephone messages on paper, Windows lets you jot them down on the Notepad instead. The Notepad is a simple text editor, which has fewer options for formatting text than Windows Write. You can perform the basic tasks for entering, editing, and selecting text just as you would in Windows Write (see Lesson 5 for review, if necessary). Windows saves Notepad files with the extension **.TXT**.

To open the Notepad,

1. Double-click on the notepad icon in the Accessories window.

In contrast to Write, the Notepad does not wrap text automatically. If you do not choose to use the Word Wrap option, your text will extend to the right far beyond the screen border, and you will need to do a great deal of scrolling. To prevent this, turn on Word Wrap when you use the Notepad.

Note: Word Wrap, a feature of all word processors, automatically brings your cursor from the right margin of a line that is full down to the left margin of the next line.

To turn on Word Wrap,

1. Open the document on your Student Data disk called **ADHOC**.
2. Choose Edit and look at the words **Word Wrap**. If they are already checked, Word Wrap is on and you can ESCAPE from the menu. If not checked, click on Word Wrap to turn it on (see Figure 6-8).

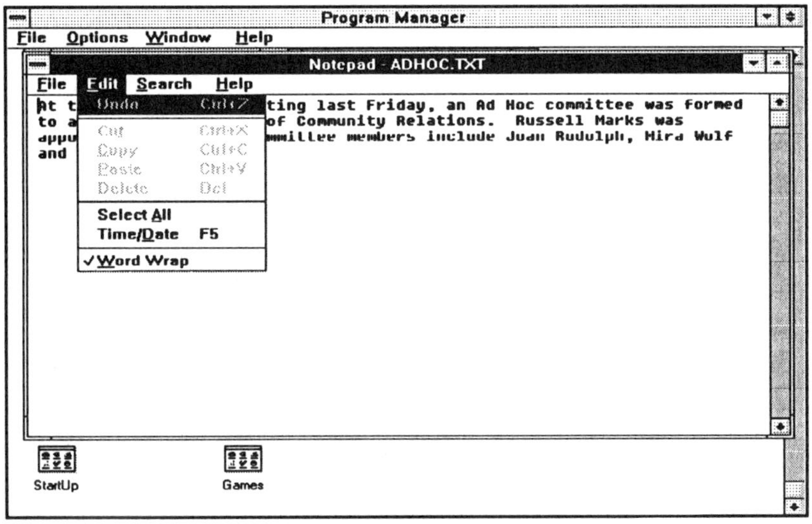

Figure 6-8: *Windows Notepad: Turning on Word Wrap*

There is an option in Notepad that allows you to select all the text in your document.

To select all text in your document,

1. Choose Edit and Select All.
2. Deselect the text by clicking anywhere on the screen.

Another special feature of the Notepad is the option of creating a Time-Log document. This adds the date and time to your document whenever you open it, giving you a clear record of exactly when you worked on the document.

To create a Time-Log document,

1. Begin a new document (hint: use the File menu).
2. At the left margin of the first line, type:

   .LOG

   You must type uppercase letters (see Figure 6-9).
3. Do not enter any text. Save the document as **LOGFILE**, using the typical Save As... procedure.
4. Open the *same file* again. You will see the current date and time.

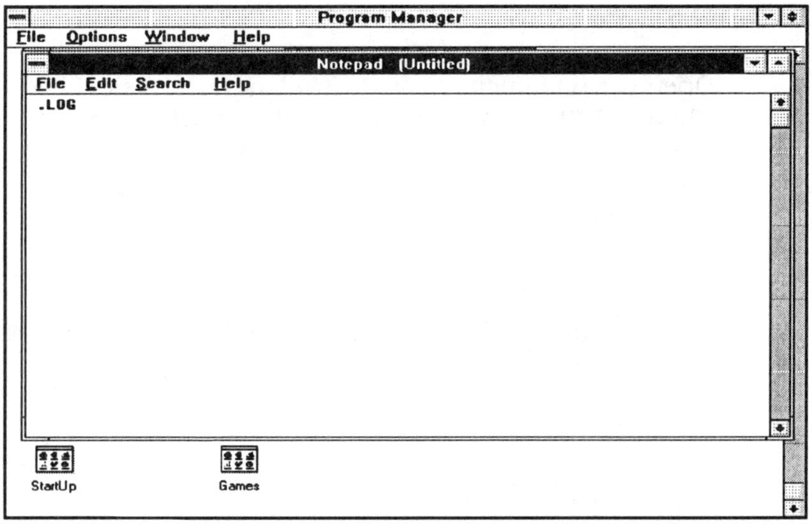

Figure 6-9: *Creating a Time-Log Document*

5. Type the following: **I am beginning to work with the Windows 3.1 Notepad.**
6. Save the file again.

Closing Exercise

1. Exit from the Notepad, using one of the typical Exit procedures.

Review Exercises

1. Open the Accessories window, if it is not already open.
2. Open the Clock. If the clock is displaying the time in analog mode, change to digital mode. Set the clock to run on top of any open windows. Minimize the clock and leave it running.
3. Open the Calendar. Open the file **MYCAL** that you created earlier in this lesson. Enter the following appointments for the week *following* the current week:

Monday	**10 AM**	**Advisement Session w/ Dr. Leonard**
Wednesday	**1 PM**	**Meet Sue for Lunch at Topsy's**
Thursday	**9 AM**	**Makeup English exam. Pratt Hall, Room 444**

   Save your calendar file and exit from the application.
4. Open the Cardfile program. Open the file called **MYCARD**. Add the following cards:

Harris Brown
United Textiles
301 East 44 St.
New York, NY 10016
(212) 555-2160

Sue Jones
97 Foxhollow Rd.
Mt. Vernon, NY 10788
(914) 645-2265

Save your file. Change to List View, look at your cards, and change back to Card View. Change the Index line of **Computer Trackers** to read:
Computer Trackers: Andy Griffen (hint: locate card and then use Edit Index...). Look up Dr. Price's telephone number. Save again and exit from the cardfile.

5. Open the Notepad and turn on Word Wrap (if it is not already on). Open the file called **LOGFILE** and notice that the current date and time have been added. Add the following entry:

   I am continuing to work with the Windows 3.1 accessories.

   Save the file and exit from the Notepad.

7

Sharing Data Among Applications

The objectives of this lesson are to

- Copy and move data from one application to another
- Review working in the Notepad, Cardfile, and Calendar

Note: Before you begin this lesson, insert your Student Data disk into the correct drive. Start Windows and open the Accessories group window. If necessary, enlarge the window so that you can see all the icons.

In Lesson 5 we learned to move and copy data in Windows Write. We can use the same procedure, with one additional step, to move or copy data from one application to another. Imagine the convenience this offers you! You can move text freely from the Notepad to the Calendar or copy an address from the cardfile to Write, with just a few simple clicks of your mouse. If you have purchased additional applications, for example Microsoft's **Excel** or **Word for Windows,** you can copy or move data from one of the simpler accessories to one of these full-featured packages and enhance it in the more complex application.

The general procedure for moving and copying data from one application to another is the same throughout the Windows environment:

1. Create the data in the first application.
2. Select the data you wish to move or copy.
3. Choose Edit Cut if you want to move the data, or Edit Copy if you wish to copy the data.
   Your data will be transferred to the Clipboard, a part of the computer's memory. It will remain in the Clipboard until something else takes its place. In the meantime, you can decide exactly where you want to place your data.
4. Switch to the second application (the one you are moving or copying *to*).
5. Position your cursor where you want the data to appear.

6. Choose Edit Paste to place your data in its new location.

We will copy a name and address from the Notepad to Windows Write.

To copy from the Notepad to Write,

1. Open the Notepad.
2. Open the Edit menu. If Word Wrap is not preceded by a check, click to turn it on.
3. Enter the following text:

   Marjorie Lyndon
   Assistant Vice President
   Mt. Kisco Savings Bank
   200 Main Street
   Mt. Kisco, NY 10549
   (914) 666-5554

4. Choose Edit and Select All (see Figure 7-1).

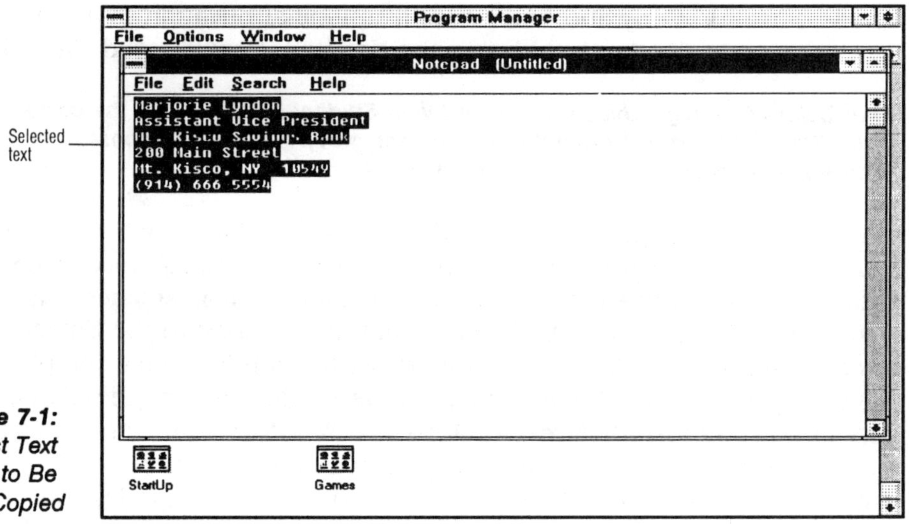

Figure 7-1: *Select Text to Be Copied*

5. Choose Edit and Copy.
6. Switch to the Program Manager (press **CTRL+ESC** to reach the Task List and double-click on Program Manager) and open Write.
7. Make sure your cursor is at the beginning of the document and choose Edit Paste.
8. Delete the line containing the telephone number.
9. Press ENTER twice and type the following text:

   I am interested in renting a safe deposit box. Please send me information on sizes, prices, and availability. Thank you very much.

Sincerely,
(your name)

10. Save your document as **DEPOSIT**.

The text you copied to Write will remain in the Clipboard until the next move or copy procedure. Since the text is still available, we can copy it more than once. Let's copy the same text to the Cardfile.

To copy from the Clipboard to the Cardfile,

1. Open the Windows Cardfile.
2. Open the file saved as **MYCARD**.
3. Choose Card and Add.
4. At the Index line, type: **Lyndon, Marjorie** and press ENTER.
5. At the blank card, choose Edit and Paste.
6. Select the first line (the duplicate name, see Figure 7-2) and DELETE.

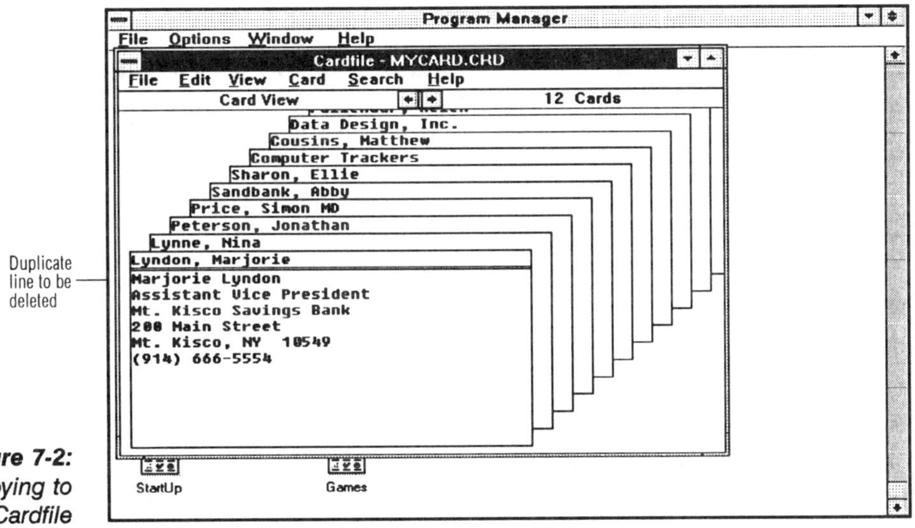

Figure 7-2: *Copying to the Cardfile*

7. Save the file and exit from the application (hint: Use the File Save and then File Exit).

Note: If you need help using the Notepad and Calendar, turn to Lesson 6. For help with Write, turn to Lesson 5.

Review Exercises

1. Open Windows, open the Accessories window, and open the Notepad.
2. Turn on Word Wrap, if it is not already on.
3. Type the following notes on the Notepad:

Call Joe tomorrow, 9AM for latest price on #37 (303) 677-7200 Ext. 443

Keith Reilly, MD
367 Central Park South
New York, NY 10032

Betty Hogan, Ganz Textiles, 534-8798

4. A. Select the lines containing Dr. Reilly's name and address.
   B. Choose Edit and Copy.
   C. Switch to the Program Manager and open Write.
   D. Paste your selected text into Write.
   E. Write a short letter to Dr. Reilly and save your file as **REILLY**.
   F. Close Write and switch back to the Notepad.

Note: DO NOT click on the notepad icon from the Accessories menu. This will open a new copy of the Notepad, not the one you used. Remember to return to the Notepad by switching to it from the Task List (CTRL+ESC).

5. A. Select the lines containing the reminder to call Joe.
   B. Choose Edit and Cut.
   C. Use the Task List to switch to the Program Manager. Open the calendar.
   D. Open the file saved as **MYCAL** and scroll ahead one day. Paste the data next to 9AM. Save your file and exit from the calendar.
   E. Use the Task List to switch back to the Notepad.
6. A. Select the lines containing the information about Betty Hogan.
   B. Choose Edit and Copy.
   C. Switch to the Program Manager and open the Cardfile.
   D. Open the file saved as **MYCARD**. Choose Card and Add.
   E. Type: **Betty Hogan** on the index line and paste the text into the new card. Delete Betty's name from the text you just copied.
   F. Save the Cardfile and exit from the application.
7. Close the Notepad without saving.
8. A. Begin a new file in the Notepad and make it a Time-Log document (hint: type **.LOG** at left margin).
   B. Save the document as **SHARE** and exit.
   C. Re-enter the document and write a short summary of what you learned in this lesson. Save the file.
9. Exit from the Notepad, using one of the methods you have learned.

8
Using the File Manager

The objectives of this lesson are to

- Understand the functions of the File Manager
- Start the File Manager
- Understand the parts of the File Manager screen
- Format a disk
- Copy a disk
- Use the Directory Tree
- Move and Copy files from the File Manager
- Delete a file from the File Manager
- Start applications from the File Manager

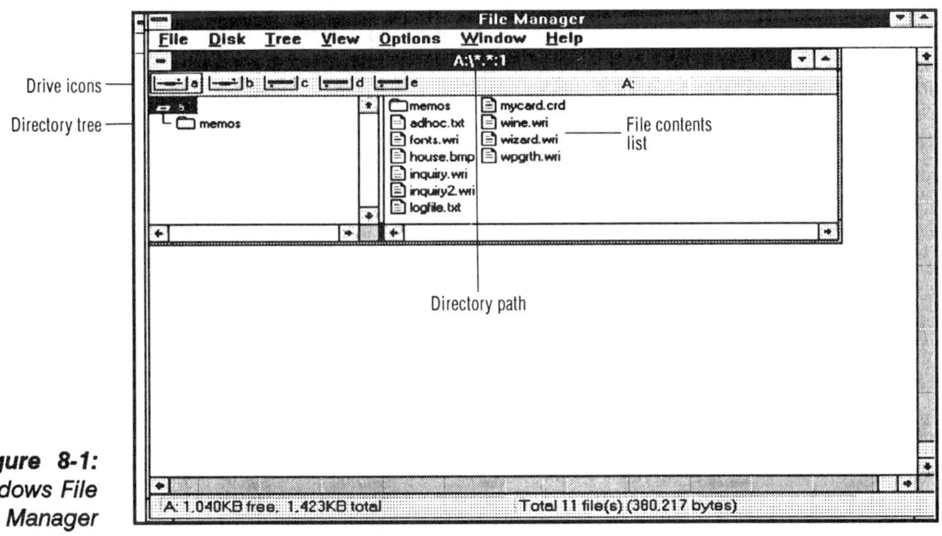

Figure 8-1: *Windows File Manager*

The Windows 3.1 File Manager (see Figure 8-1) helps you organize and maintain your files and disks without having to leave the Windows environment. With the File Manager, you can accomplish many of the file and disk management tasks normally done in DOS. In addition, File Manager provides another way of starting both Windows and non-Windows applications. The File Manager icon can be found in the Main program group.

As you can see, the File Manager screen is complex. We will examine one section at time.

To start File Manager,

1. Start Windows, if it is not running.
2. Open the Main program group window (if it is not open already). If necessary, resize the window so you can see all the icons.
3. Double-click on the File Manager icon. It looks like a filing cabinet.
4. To make sure that your View is correct, open the View menu. If a check (✓) precedes **Tree and Directory**, you can ESCAPE. Otherwise, click on **Tree and Directory** to select it.

Understanding the Directory Tree

When you open the File Manager, you will see a screen containing two windows, one inside the other. The outer window displays the application name, **File Manager**, with its menu directory below. The next line lists the *drives* on your computer, for example **a:** and **c:** or **a:**, **b:**, and **c:**. Underneath the drives, the inner window is divided in half. You can move or resize the inner window without changing the outer one.

The left half of the inner window is the **Directory Tree.** Directories divide a drive into sections and allow the user to save files that belong together in the same place. The Directory Tree always shows the root directory, for example **a:** or **c:**. It may also show other directories on the selected drive. One of the directories in the Directory Tree window will always be selected—either highlighted, if that part of the window is active, or enclosed in a box if it is not.

The right half of the inner window displays the **File Contents List**, a list of files contained in the selected directory . Each time you select a different directory (by clicking on it) the File Contents List will change to show the files contained in that directory.

The Title Bar of the inner window displays the **Directory Path**, which is the DOS description of the files on the File Contents List.

The following table summarizes these elements of the File Manager:

Directory Path	Found in the Title Bar of the inner window. Always describes the files listed in the File Contents List.
Directory Tree	Contains a list of directories on the active drive, beginning with the root directory. You can display the entire structure of the drive, or only the parts you need. The current directory is the one selected, and it will have its files listed on the Contents list.
File Contents List	Contains a listing of files in the currently selected directory. Each filename is accompanied by one of four icons, representing different types of files.
Drive Icons	An icon representing each disk drive is found above the Directory Tree. The active drive is enclosed by a square and is found next to the icons.

Table 8-1: *Elements of the File Manager*

Note: Before you begin this exercise, insert your Student Data disk into the correct drive. Start Windows and open the Main group window. If necessary, make the window bigger so that you can see all the icons.

To View the structure of a disk,

1. Click on the drive icon for the drive containing your Student Data disk.
   The Directory Tree will now display the structure of your Student Data disk (see Figure 8-2).

Structure of disk

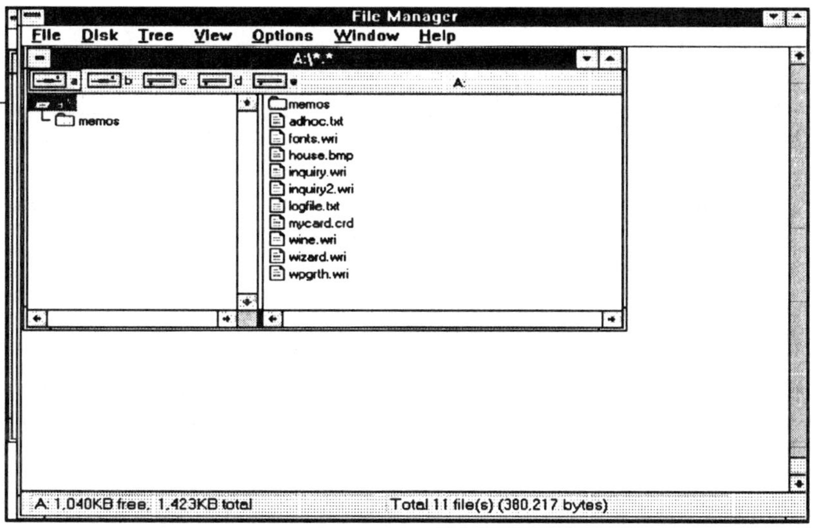

Figure 8-2: *Structure of the Student Data Disk*

2. Click once on the *root directory* (**a:** or **b:**) to make it active.

Note: Do not double-click on the root directory or your Directory Tree display may change.

Note: Do not double-click on a drive icon or a second Directory window will open. If this happens, close it by double-clicking on its control menu box.

The Directory Tree shows that the Student Data disk contains both a root directory and a directory called **memos**. You can tell that the root directory is active because the file folder next to it is open and highlighted.
The Title Bar tells you which files from the selected directory are listed below (***.*** means that *all* files in the root directory of the Student Data disk are listed).
The File Contents List shows all the filenames in the directory.

3. Click on the **memos** directory to select it. Now the icon next to **memos** is an open file folder and the one next to the root directory is a closed file (see Figure 8-3).

The root directory is expanded

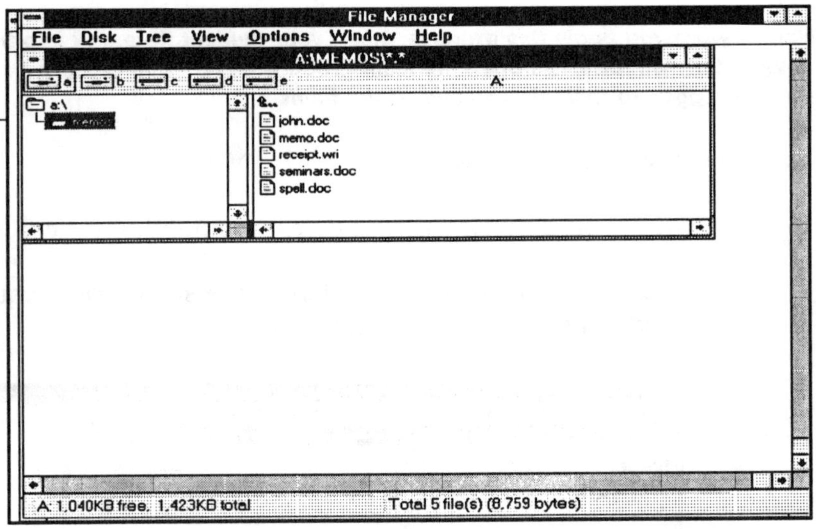

Figure 8-3: *Selecting a Different Directory*

Notice that the file list has changed. Now the files you see listed are the ones saved in the **memos** directory. The Title Bar has changed also, to reflect the new file listing.

Expanding and Collapsing Directories

If you look back at the icon for the root directory (**a:** or **b:**), you will see that it contains a **minus**. The minus is very difficult to see so look closely at the open file folder or see Figure 8-3. The minus means that the directory contains one or more other directories, and that those directories are currently displayed. The root directory is *expanded*. Removing the display of the expanded directories is called *collapsing* a directory.

Note: If you cannot see the minus sign, choose Tree from the menu and click on Indicate Expandable Branches.

To collapse a directory,

1. Double-click on the minus sign on the root directory.

The **memos** directory is no longer displayed and the icon on the root directory has changed from a minus to a plus.

To expand a directory,

1. Double-click on the plus sign on the root directory.
   The **memos** directory is displayed again.

Note: You may also use the Tree menu to expand and collapse directory listings.

Opening a Second Directory Tree Window

We are currently looking at the structure of the drive containing the Student Data disk. There are two ways to see the structure of a different drive.

1. Click on the icon for a second drive to *change* the displayed drive.
2. Double-click on the icon for a second drive to open an *additional* Directory Tree window.

To open a second Directory Tree window,

1. Double-click on the icon for the hard drive (usually **c:**)
   A second Directory Tree window will open (see Figure 8-4).
2. Use your ability to move and resize windows to arrange the two directory tree windows directly under each other (see Figure 8-5).

Note: If you prefer, you can use the Window menu to open a second Directory Tree window. To do so, choose Window and New Window.

3. To close one of the windows, double-click on its control menu box.

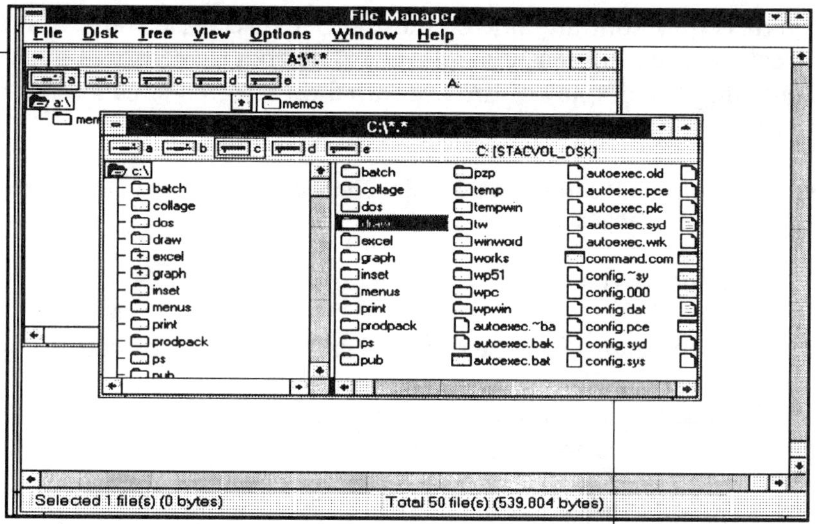

Figure 8-4: *Opening a Second Directory Tree Window*

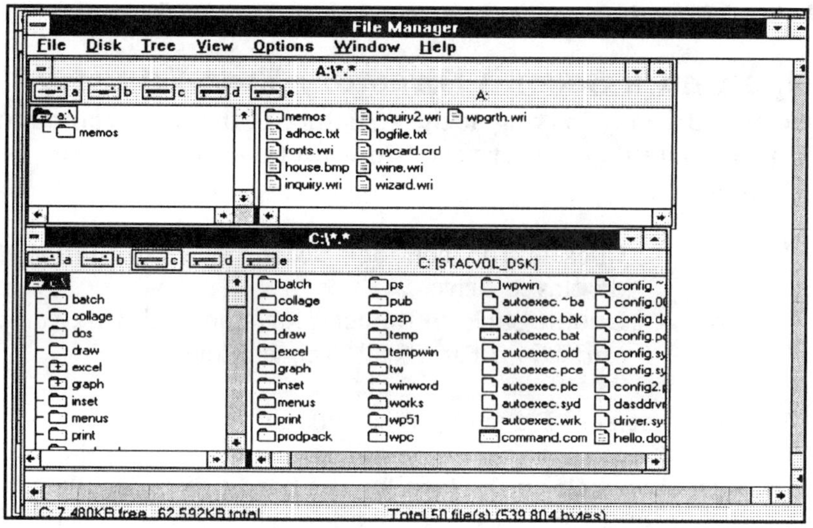

Figure 8-5: *Arranging Your Directory Tree Windows*

Using the File Manager Menus

The File Manager menu can be used to manage disks and files, get Help, and control the display of directories and files.

Creating a Directory

There are times when you need to create a new directory. Each directory you create must have a *parent*, or directory that it belongs to. The parent of **memos** is the root directory of your Student Data disk.

Look at the Directory Tree window. Notice how **memos** is listed below and slightly to the right of its parent directory. All directories that share the same parent will be listed directly underneath each other, and Windows will automatically place them in alphabetical order.

To create a directory,

1. Make sure that the root directory of your Student Data disk (**a:** or **b:**) is selected (see Figure 8-6).

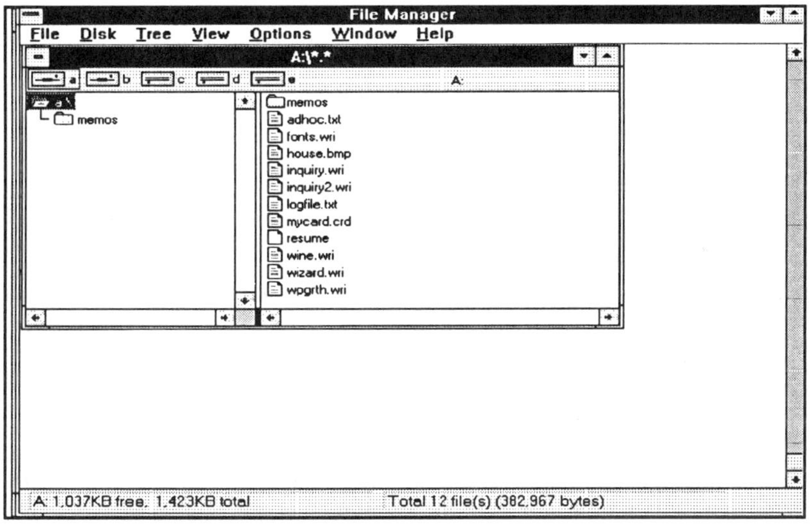

Figure 8-6: *Ready to Create a Directory*

2. Choose File and Create Directory from the menu.
3. When the Create Directory dialog box appears, check that the directory listed is **a:** or **b:**. If not, cancel and click on **a:** or **b:**.
4. Type: **BUDGET** as the name for your new directory. Directory names must follow the same rules as filenames (no more than 8 characters, no spaces allowed).
5. Choose OK. Your directory tree should look like Figure 8-7.

To change directories,

1. Click on **budget**. You will see that no files are listed. The two dots and up arrow that are displayed on the file list are a shortcut to the parent directory. The dots and arrow are called the **Up Icon**.
2. Double-click on the **Up Icon** to switch back to the parent directory.

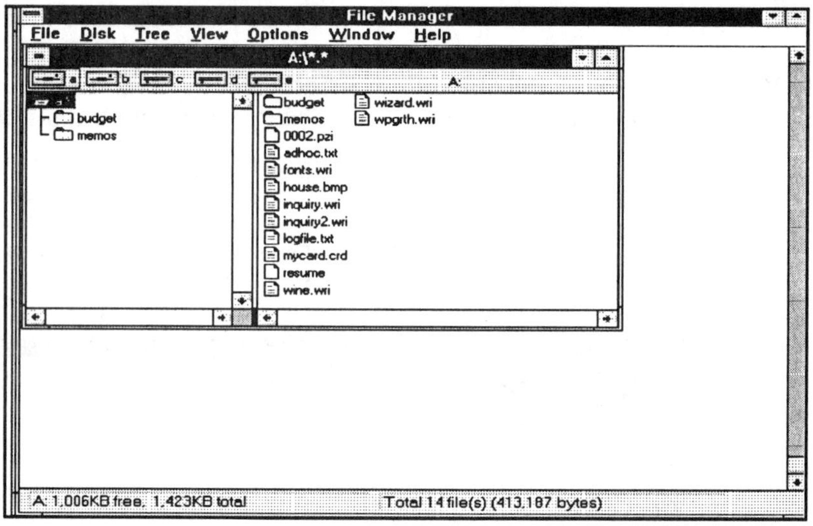

Figure 8-7: *File Manager with New Directory Displayed*

Formatting a Disk

When you are working in Windows, there are times when you need to format a disk. The format procedure prepares a disk for use. You cannot save files on a disk that has not been formatted. It is easy to format a disk from the File Manager Disk menu.

Note: DO NOT use your Student Data disk in the following exercise or you will erase all files on that disk. For the following exercise, obtain another disk, which is either new or contains files you are sure you will not need again.

To format a disk from the File Manager disk menu,

1. Place a new disk or one containing files you do not mind erasing in the appropriate drive.
   Do not use your Student Data disk for this exercise!
2. Choose Disk and Format Disk from the menu.
3. If necessary, open the list box next to the words **Disk In** so the drive containing your disk to be formatted is listed.
4. Click on OK (unless your instructor tells you otherwise).
5. Read the confirmation message. When you are sure that you will not be losing important files by formatting your disk, click on Yes.
6. Watch the dialog box, which informs you about the progress of the format procedure. You can cancel at any time.
7. You will see a dialog box asking you if you want to format another disk. Answer **No.** Your formatting procedure is complete.

Sometimes you need to make a duplicate copy of a disk. It is always a good idea to make a copy of an important disk, in case something happens to your working copy. You can do this from the File Manager with the Copy Disk command. The Copy Disk command will work only if you are copying to a second disk of the same size and format. In the Copy Disk procedure:

- The disk you are copying *from* is the *source disk.*
- The disk you are copying *to* is the *destination disk.*

Place the source disk in one drive and the destination disk in another drive of the same size.

If you don't have two drives of the same size and capacity, don't be afraid to use the same drive as *both* your source and destination. In that case, begin with the source disk in the drive and follow the screen prompts for removing the source and inserting the destination disk in its place.

To copy a disk from the File Manager menu,

1. Write-protect the Student Data disk (move the hard tab on the back so that it is flush with the bottom of the disk and the hole is not covered).

Note: DO NOT attempt the following exercise until you have write-protected your Student Data disk. When you complete the exercise you may remove the write-protection.

2. Remove the disk you formatted in the last exercise and insert your Student Data disk in its place.
3. Choose Disk and Copy Disk from the menu.
   The Student Data disk is the *source disk*.
   The newly formatted disk is the *destination disk*.
4. Make sure the box next to the words **Source In** and the box next to **Destination** list the drives containing your disks. If you are using only one disk drive, both boxes should indicate the drive containing your Student Data disk. Remember that your source and destination disks MUST be the same size and capacity.
5. Choose OK.
6. When the Confirm box appears, reminding you that any data on your destination diskette will be erased, choose **Yes.**
7. You will be prompted to insert your source disk. Since it is already in the drive, choose OK.
   Watch the dialog box.
8. If necessary, follow the prompt to insert your destination disk.
9. Follow any additional prompts until the copy disk process is complete.
10. Remove the newly copied disk and label it (a folder of adhesive-backed labels is included with every box of new disks).

11. Remove the write-protection from your Student Data disk and replace the disk in your computer.

Moving and Copying Files

Windows allows you to move or copy single files or groups of files from one directory to another by clicking on the file icon(s) and dragging the file(s) to a different directory. This method is called **Drag and Drop**. If you prefer, you can use the file menu to move and copy.

To move a file from one directory to another,

1. Make the root directory of your Student Data disk active (on the Directory Tree, click on a:\ or b:\).
2. At the File Contents List, click on the file called **resume**, keeping your finger down on the mouse button.
3. Drag the mouse pointer toward the Directory Tree. It will look as though a document is attached to the pointer.
4. At the Directory Tree, position the pointer directly on top of the budget directory listing and release the mouse button.
5. You should a see a dialog box asking you if you want to move the selected file(s) to the **budget** directory. Answer **Yes**.
   Look at the file list—**resume** is gone!
6. Click on the **budget** directory. It now has one file—**resume**.

To copy a file,

1. Again, select the root directory of your Student Data disk.
2. Press the **CTRL** key and hold it down.
3. At the File Contents List, click on the file called **wpgrth.wri** and drag it across to the **budget** directory listing.
4. When the file is directly on top of **budget**, release both hands.
5. The Confirmation message should indicate that you are *copying* a file to the **budget** directory. Answer **Yes**.
   Since you have copied and not moved the file, **wpgrth.wri** still appears on the file list.
6. Click on the **budget** directory. It now has two files, **resume** and **wpgrth.wri**.

Moving and Copying Groups of Files

The procedure for moving or copying more than one file is exactly the same as moving or copying a single file. Before you move or copy, however, you must select the files. Sometimes the group of files will be listed in sequence, but at other times they will be scattered throughout the file contents list.

To select files in sequence,

1. Again, select the root directory of your Student Data disk.
2. Click on **adhoc.txt**.
3. Hold down the **SHIFT** key and click on **deposit.wri**. **Adhoc, deposit,** and any files in between will be selected (see Figure 8-8).

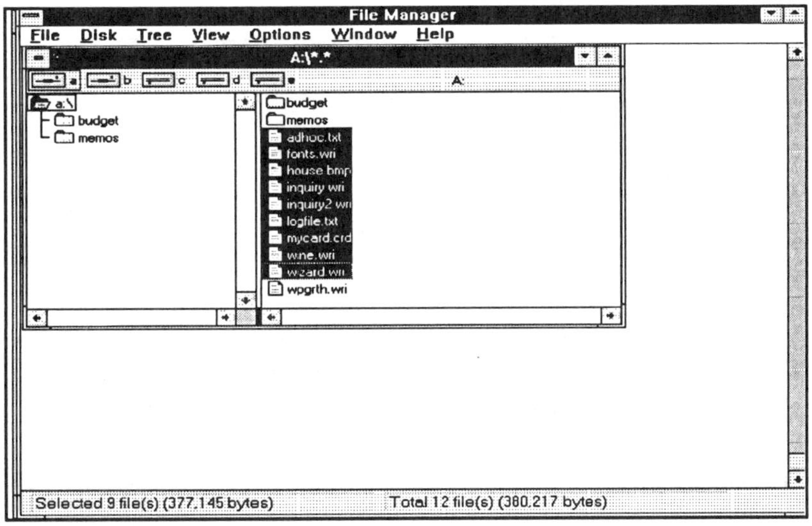

Figure 8-8: *Files Selected in Sequence*

4. Press **CTRL**, point to *any* of the highlighted files, and drag them to the **budget** directory to copy the files. If you get a dialog box asking you to confirm File Replace, click on Yes.

To select files not in sequence,

1. Remove the selection from the last group of files by clicking anywhere on the selected block.
2. Click on **adhoc.txt**.
3. Hold down the **CTRL** key and click on **inquiry.wri**, **wine.wri**, and **wpgrth.wri.** Each file you clicked on will be selected.
4. To remove the selection of **inquiry**, hold down **CTRL** and click on it.
5. To remove the selection of all files but one, click on **wpgrth.wri** without holding down **CTRL**. That file will remain selected and all other selected files will be deselected.

Deleting Files and Directories

When you have no further need for a file or directory you can delete it. Deleting unwanted files and directories keeps your disks better organized and makes space available for new files. To delete a file in the File Manager, select it and press the **DELETE** key. To delete a directory, you must first remove all files from the directory. Then, select the directory and press **DELETE**.

To delete a file,

1. Click on the **budget** directory to make it active.
2. Select the file **wpgrth.wri**.
3. Press **DELETE.** If the Delete dialog boxes contain the correct information, click on OK and then on Yes (see Figure 8-9).

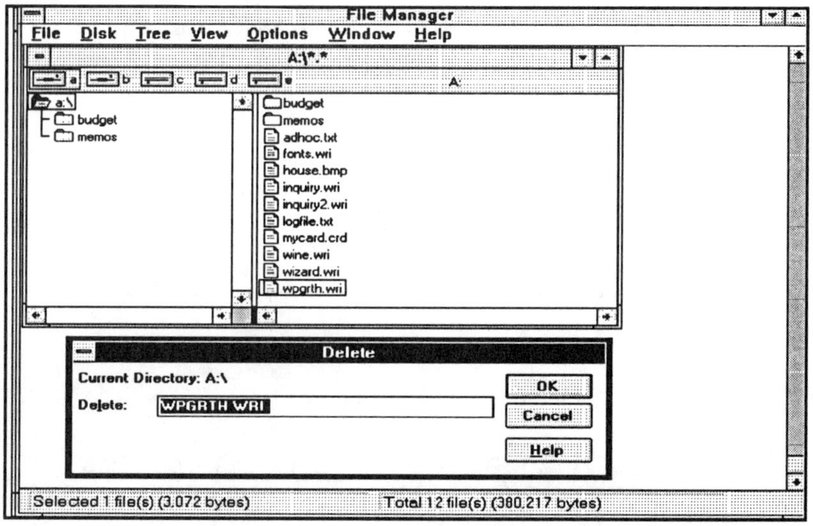

Figure 8-9: *Delete Confirmation Box*

Note: If you do not see the Delete dialog box, choose Options and Confirmation from the menu. At the Confirmation dialog box, click on File Delete. This turns on the command that will allow you to confirm each file deletion.

To delete a directory,

1. Click on the file **adhoc.txt**. Press **SHIFT** and click on the last file on your list. Drag the files to the **memos** directory and confirm that you want to move them there.
2. The **budget** directory is now empty. Select it and press **DELETE**.
3. If the Delete dialog boxes contain the correct information, click on OK and Yes to all.

Launching Applications from File Manager

If you are in File Manager, you do not have to return to the Program Manager to start another application.

We have seen how File Manager can list the files on any drive. When you want to start an application, first make the drive and directory containing that application active. You will see all the files for that application on your File Contents list. Find the exact file that starts the application and double-click on it. The application will open.

Note: The file that starts a program will usually consist of the name of the program and the extension, .exe or .com.

To open the Notepad from the File Manager,

1. Click on the icon of the drive that contains your Windows directory (probably **c:** — if not, ask your instructor for help.)
2. Scroll the list of directories and select the **windows** directory.
3. Scroll the File Contents list and double-click on the file **notepad.exe** (see Figure 8-10). This file will launch the Notepad.

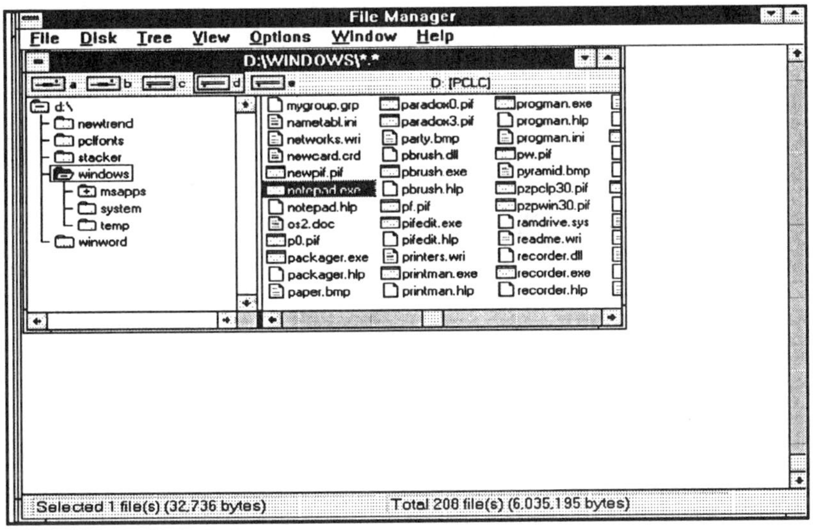

Figure 8-10: *Ready to Start the Notepad*

4. The Notepad will open. Type a few words.
5. Close the Notepad without saving.
6. The File Manager will still be running.

Note: If File Manager automatically minimizes, open the Options menu. Look for a check (✓) next to Minimize on Use. Click on this option to deselect it.

Save Settings on Exit

When you leave the File Manager, you can choose to keep your current settings by checking **Save Settings on Exit** on the Options menu. By *not* choosing this option, you can always enter File Manager with the same unchanged settings.

Closing Exercise

1. Close the File Manager, using one of the methods you have learned. *Do not* check Save Settings on Exit.

Review Exercises

1. A. Open the File Manager.
   B. Obtain a new disk and format it.

2. A. Remove the newly formatted disk and replace it with the Student Data disk. Make sure the root directory (**a:** or **b:**) is active.
   B. Make the drive containing your Student Data disk active. Create a new directory called **temp**.
3. A. Make the **memos** directory active.
   B. Select the first file, **john.doc**. Copy the file to the **temp** directory.
   C. Click on **temp** to make sure the file has been copied.
4. A. Click on the **memos** directory again to select it.
   B. Select the files **receipt.wri** and **spell.doc**.
   C. Move the files to the **temp directory**.
   D. Click on **temp** to make sure the files have been moved.
5. A. Click on **memos** again.
   B. Select the remaining files and copy them to the root directory of your Student Data disk. Click on Yes to replace the files.
6. A. Delete all files in **memos.**
   B. Delete the **memos** directory.
   C. Select the temp directory and use the file menu to rename it **newmemos** (hint: use File and Rename).
7. A. Double-click on the icon representing the drive containing your Windows directory to open a second Directory Tree window.
   B. Move and size the new window so you can see both directory trees and file lists.
   C. At the second window, scroll the list of directories. Click on several of them and watch the file contents list change.
8. A. Click on the **windows** directory.
   B. Scroll the file list and watch for all files with the extension **.exe**. Each of these files will start one of the Windows accessories.
   C. Start the calculator (hint:double-click on **calc.exe**).
   D. Switch back to the File Manager (hint: click on the File Manager window if it is visible or use the Task List).
   E. Start the Cardfile.
9. A. Close the Cardfile, File Manager, and Calculator.

9

Using the Control Panel

The objectives of this lesson are to

- Understand the functions managed by the Control Panel
- Change screen colors
- Customize the desktop
- Use the screen saver
- Change the mouse controls

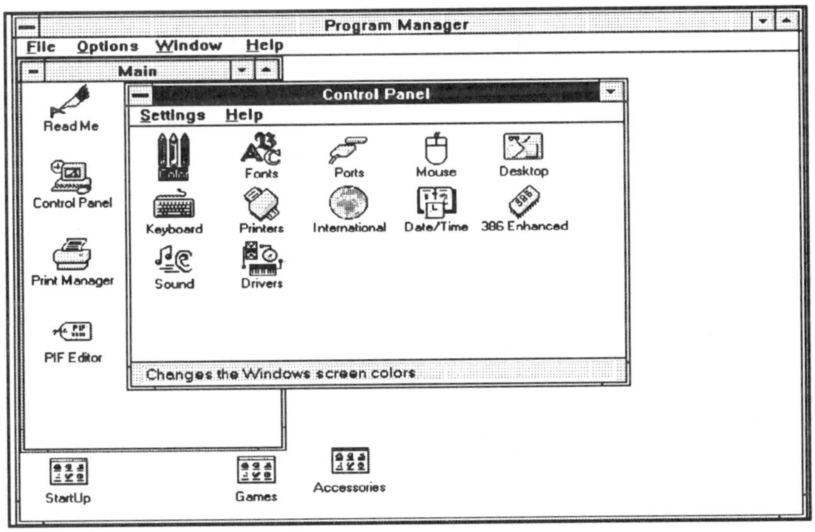

Figure 9-1: *Windows Control Panel*

The Control Panel (see Figure 9-1) is located within the Main program group window. It contains a number of programs, several new to Windows 3.1, that let you customize the appearance and settings of Windows on your system. Two of these functions, Color and Desktop, let you control the appearance of your screen. Some icons (for example, the network icon) will not appear on the Control Panel unless your hardware and/or software support them. The other icons allow you to update your hardware information or your system settings. Any settings you choose or change in the Control Panel will be available throughout the Windows environment.

To open the Control Panel,

1. Open Windows.
2. Open the Main program group.
3. Double-click on the Control Panel icon.

We will look at three of the Control Panel programs in this lesson—Color, Desktop, and Mouse. Printers will be discussed in Appendix B. The remaining features are:

Fonts	Adds or removes soft fonts, cartridges, and True Type fonts used in Windows applications.
Ports	Defines the settings for each of the communication ports.
386 Enhanced	Appears only if you are operating in 386 enhanced mode; allows you to set the defaults that determine how to allocate resources among simultaneously running programs.
International	Changes the date, time, currency, number format, and other settings that typically vary from country to country.
Keyboard	Controls the key repeat rate.
Date/Time	Resets the computer's date and time.
Drivers	Installs and configures the drivers for devices that are optional.
Network	Controls your connection to the network, including user id and password; appears only if you use Windows on a network.
Sound	Turns the warning beep off and on.

Table 9-1: *Remaining Features of the Control Panel*

Changing the Windows Color Scheme

Windows uses color to differentiate elements of the screen such as the desktop, active and inactive windows, and title bar. If you don't like the color scheme presently in use, Windows provides additional preset schemes you may choose instead. Many new color schemes have been added with the introduction of Windows 3.1.

To change to another color scheme,

1. Double-click on the color icon on the Control Panel screen.
2. Look at the name of the color scheme presently listed, so that you can return to it later.
3. Open the list box of color schemes by clicking on the down arrow.
4. Scroll the list and click on the scheme called **Black Leather Jacket** (see Figure 9-2). Note the color change directly below the list.

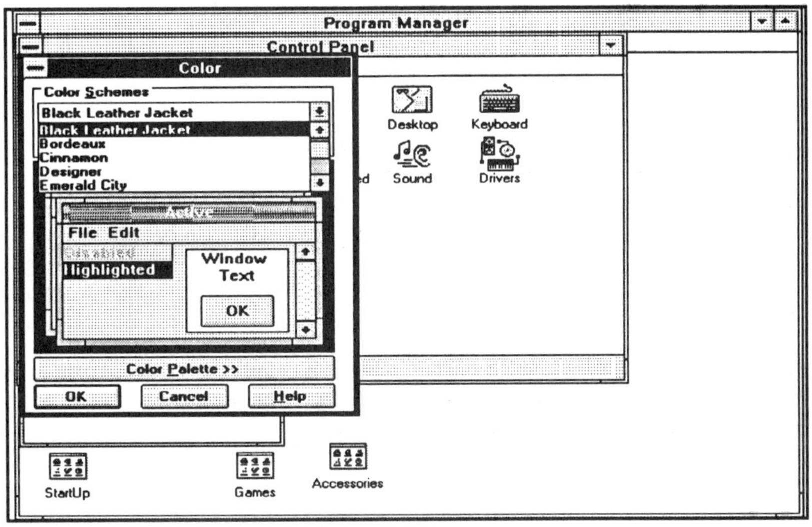

Figure 9-2: *Changing the Color Scheme*

5. Open the list again and click on **Emerald City**.
6. Open the list one more time and click on **Rugby**. If necessary, scroll the listing. Do not click on OK.
7. Close the Color dialog box by double-clicking on its control menu box.

Using the Desktop

Windows provides additional ways to customize the appearance of your screen. The Desktop program allows you to choose a pattern or wallpaper as the desktop background, rather than a solid color. It also allows you to choose a screen saver, change the rate at which your cursor blinks, adjust the space between icons, and change the border width of your window frames.

To choose a Pattern background,

1. From the Control Panel window, double-click on the Desktop icon.
2. Open the **Pattern** list box, scroll the list and click on **Scottie** (see Figure 9-3).
   Be sure that **Wallpaper**, (the third division in the box), is set to **None** (hint: scroll upward to **None** and click).

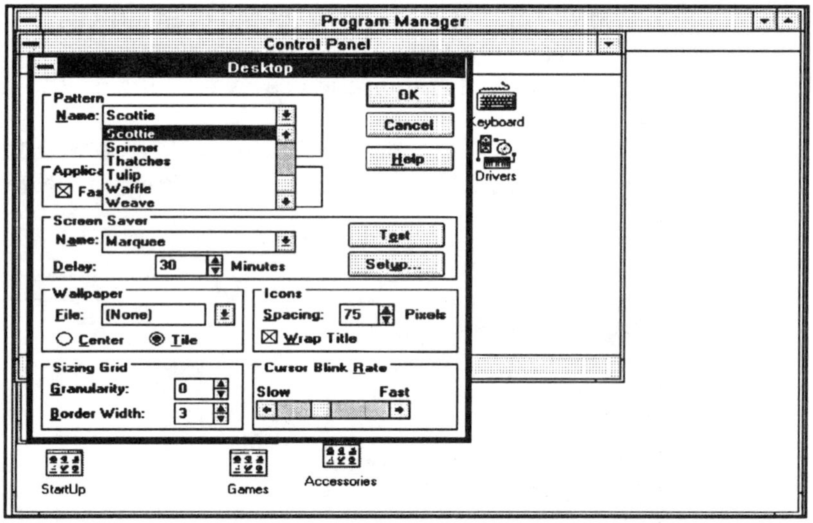

Figure 9-3: *Choosing a Pattern for the Desktop*

3. To see the pattern, click on OK.

Note: If you cannot see the pattern, there is probably a window in the way. Click on the Restore button of any maximized window to reduce its size. Now you will be able to see the background pattern of Scotties.

To choose a Wallpaper design,

1. From the Control Panel window, double-click on the desktop icon.
2. Open the **Pattern** list box again, scroll the list *upward*, and click on **None.**
3. Click on the **Tile** option button (in the Wallpaper section of the screen) so your Wallpaper will cover the desktop.
4. Open the **Wallpaper** list box, scroll the list, and click on **cars**.
5. To see the wallpaper, click on OK.
6. To remove the wallpaper, double-click on the desktop icon. Open the Wallpaper list box, scroll the list *upward*, and click on **None**. Click on OK.

Using the Screen Saver

A screen saver is a moving pattern that will appear on your monitor after your computer has not been touched for a specified interval. It will prevent damage caused by the image "burning" into the screen.

To use the screen saver,

1. From the Control Panel window, double-click on the desktop icon.

2. Open the **Screen Saver** list box.
3. Click on **Flying Windows** (see Figure 9-4).

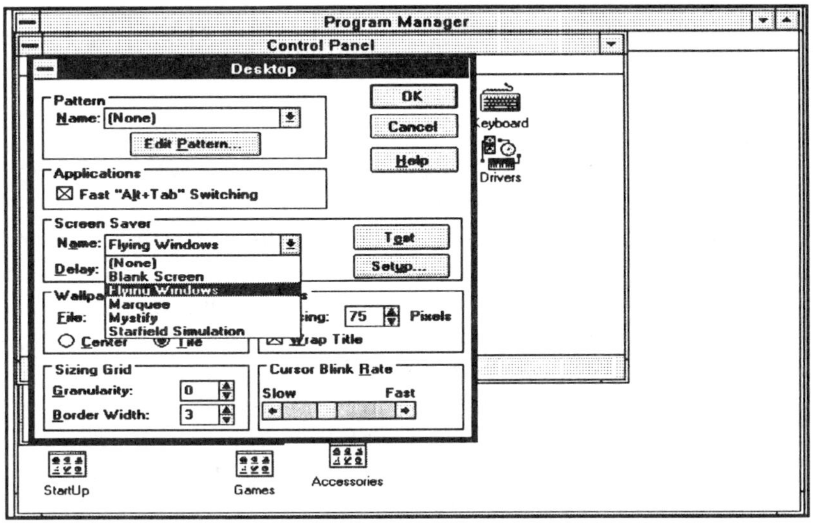

Figure 9-4: *Setting up a Screen Saver*

4. Click on the delay box and type: **30**. The Flying Windows screen saver will turn on after you have not touched your computer for 30 minutes.
5. To see what the screen saver will look like, click on **Test**.
6. To end the test, touch any key.
7. Close the Desktop.

Changing the Border Width

If you have trouble resizing your windows, it may be hard for you to position your mouse on the window frame. You can change the width of your window frames from the Desktop dialog box.

To change the border width,

1. From the Control Panel window, double-click on the Desktop icon.
   At the bottom of the dialog box you will see a setting for border width. Note the current width so you can return to it.
2. Change the setting to **9**, by clicking on one of the triangles.
3. Click on OK.
   At the Control Panel window, notice the difference in the window frame. The change in size will affect all windows, but not dialog boxes.
4. Double-click on the desktop icon and return the border width to its former setting. Click on OK.

Closing Exercise

1. Close the Desktop and any other programs from the Control Panel that remain open.
2. Close the Control Panel.
3. Close Windows.

Review Exercises

1. A. Open Windows. Open the Control Panel and the Colors box.
   B. Write down the current color scheme.
   C. Change to the color scheme called **Plasma Power Saver**.
2. A. Use the Desktop to change the wallpaper to **Chess**. Make sure it is tiled. If **Chess** is not available, choose another wallpaper pattern.
3. A. Change the border width to **7.**
   B. Change the cursor blink rate to **Slow**.
4. A. Set the Screen Saver as follows:
   - Change the screen saver to **Marquee.**
   - Set a delay of 1 minute.
   - Click on Setup.
   - Type the text you would like to appear on your screen when your Screen Saver is working.
   - Set the position to Random.
   - Click on the right arrow in the Speed box to set the speed to Slow.
   - Choose Format Text and choose a size of 18 points and the color Lime.
   - Exit from the Format box. Exit from the Setup box.
   - Exit from the Desktop.
5. A. Don't touch the computer for 1 minute. You should see the screen saver operate.

6 A. Touch any key to return to the Desktop.
   B. Change the message of your screen saver.
   C. Exit from the Desktop.

7. A. Return all Control Panel options to their former settings.
8. A. Exit from the Control Panel.

10

Creating a New Program Group

The objectives of this lesson are to

- Create a new program group
- Add program items to the group
- Change program item properties
- Use the Window 3.1 Startup group

As we have seen in Lesson 3, the Windows Program Manager displays your applications, which are organized into group windows. These group windows, called Program Groups, are listed under the Window menu of the Program Manager and are represented by icons.

You are not limited to the program groups installed with Windows. You can create a new program group at any time and add the applications you want to it. The applications you add to your new program group may appear only in that group, or they may also appear in other groups. If you find that one of your program groups is not useful to you, you may delete it.

You can also move or copy an application from one program group to another with the Windows **Drag and Drop** technique.

To create a new program group,

1. Open Windows.
2. Open the Program Manager window.
3. Choose File and New from the menu.
4. At the dialog box, choose Program Group and OK.
5. At the next dialog box, type: **Mygroup**. This will be the name of your new program group. Leave the Group File box empty. Windows will create this file for you and will add a **.GRP** extension.
6. Click on OK. The new program group window, Mygroup, will appear (see Figure 10-1).

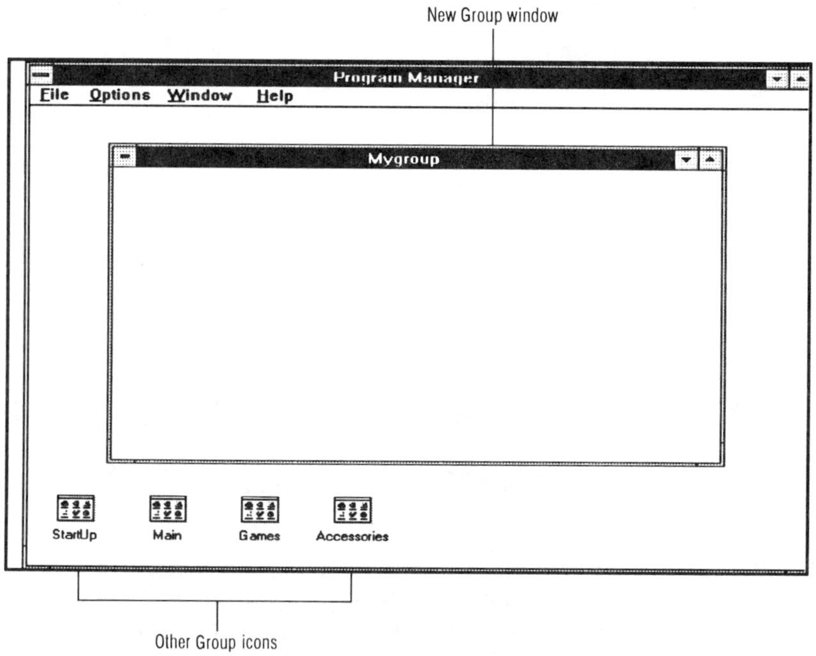

Figure 10-1: *A New Program Group*

Now that we have a new program group, we can add icons to it. Each icon we add to a program group window is called a *program item.* These icons typically represent two kinds of files:

Applications (may be Windows or non-Windows applications)	Write, WordPerfect, Excel, Cardfile, etc.
Datafiles	A commonly used file *created in one of the applications*, such as your personal calendar or a particular spreadsheet. Windows will automatically associate this document with its parent application and open them together.

Table 10-1: *Types of Program Items*

One way of adding program items to a group window is by creating them.

To create a new program item from an application,

1. Open the new group window, Mygroup.
2. Choose File and New from the Program Manager menu.

3. At the New Program Object dialog box, choose Program Item and OK.
4. At the next dialog box, type **Notepad** as your description. The description you type will appear as the name below the icon in the group window (see Figure 10-2).

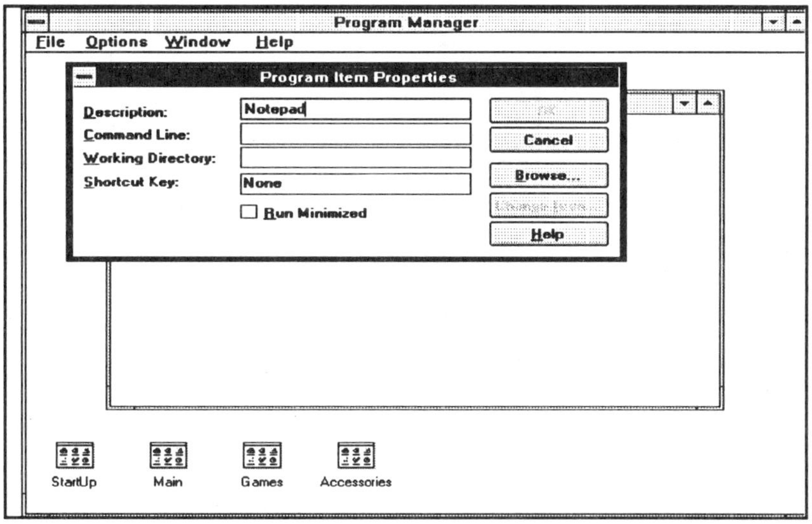

Figure 10-2: *Adding a Program Item to a Program Group*

5. Press **TAB** to move to the next line.
   At the command line, you are supposed to type the *complete* filename of the program item, including its extension and entire path.
6. Since we do not have this information, we will click on the gray button labeled **Browse...**
   The Browse dialog box automatically opens to the directory that contains Windows. It lists the program files (files that run applications) in the Windows directory (see Figure 10-3).
7. Scroll the list and click on **notepad.exe**. This is the file that runs Notepad.
8. Click on OK. You will return to the Program Menu Properties dialog box.
   It is not necessary to include a working directory or shortcut key combination.
9. Click on OK. The notepad icon will now appear in the Mygroup window.

The second type of program item you can add to your group is a datafile. A datafile that has been created in an application will open *both its own file and the application it belongs to.*
To create a new program item from a datafile,

1. Make sure that the new group window, Mygroup is open and active.

Files that run programs

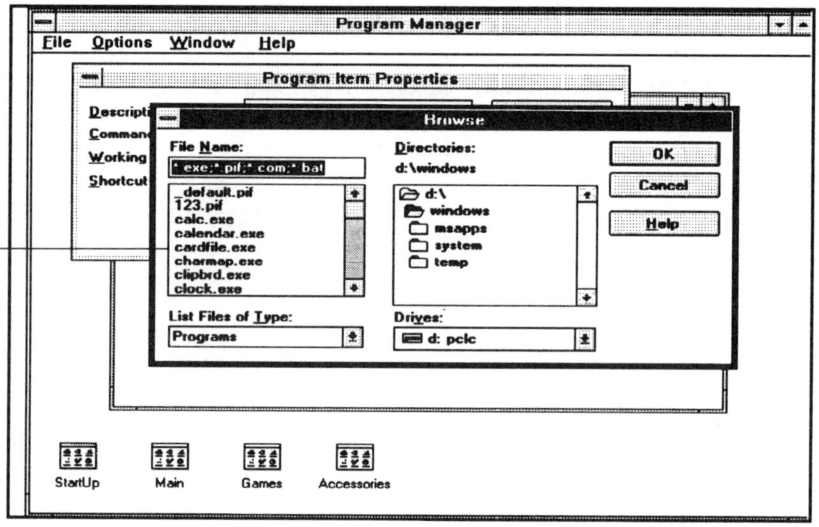

Figure 10-3: *The Browse Dialog Box*

2. Choose File and New from the Program Manager menu.
3. At the dialog box, choose Program Item and OK.
4. At the description, type: **Logfile**
5. Press **TAB** to move to the next line.
6. At the command line, type the path for the cardfile you worked with in Lesson 6.
   Depending on which drive contains your Student Data disk, type either:
   a:\logfile.txt or **b:\logfile.txt**
   (See Figure 10-4.)

Path for data file

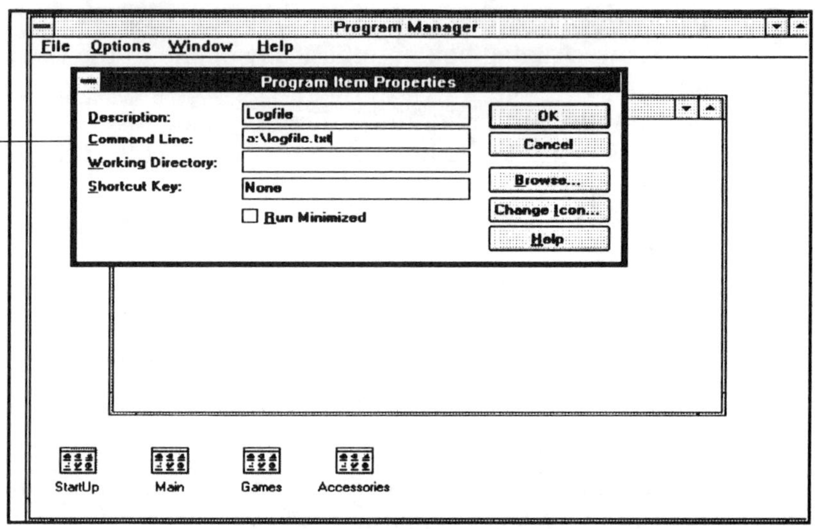

Figure 10-4: *Creating a Datafile Icon*

7. Click on OK.

The warning from Windows that says that you have specified a removable file means that the cardfile will be available to you only when your floppy disk has been inserted.

8. Answer **Yes**.
   Now you will see two icons in your new program group. When you double-click on Logfile the Notepad application will open and your own document will open with it.
   You now have two ways to open the Notepad, an application icon and a datafile icon.
9. Double-click on the Notepad icon.
   Notice the fact that it opens with a blank screen. Type a few words.
10. Close the Notepad without saving.
11. Double-click on the logfile icon.
    The Notepad opens again but this time logfile opens too. Type a few words.
12. Save your file and close the Notepad.

A third way to add a program item is to move or copy it from another program group.

To copy a program item,

1. Make sure the new group window, Mygroup, is open (see Figure 10-5).

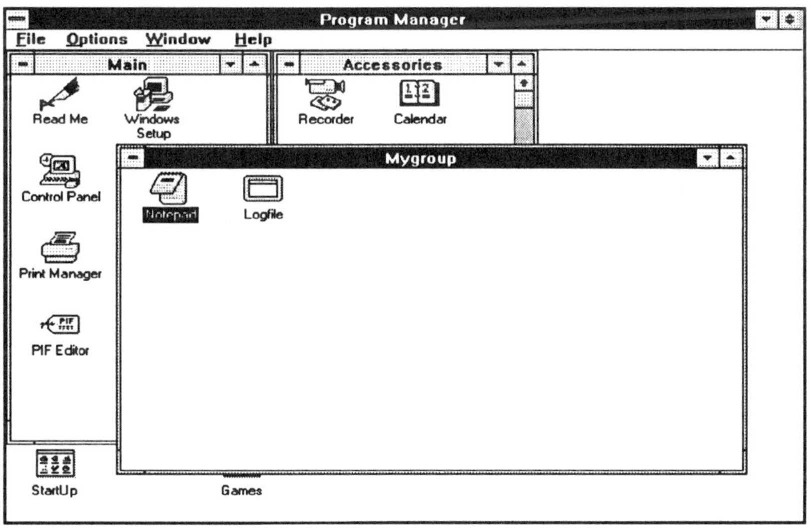

Figure 10-5: *Mygroup*

2. Open the Accessories group window also.
3. Move and size the two windows so that they are next to each other.
4. Scroll the Accessories window so that the Write icon is visible.
5. Hold down the **CTRL** key.

6. Drag the icon for Windows Write from the Accessories window to the Mygroup window.

The icon now appears in both windows and you can start Write from either one. If you had *not* depressed the **CTRL** key, you would have *moved*, not *copied* the application from Accessories to Mygroup.

Changing Program Group and Program Item Properties

The descriptions, icons, and command line information for program groups and items are called *properties* of those entities. You can change properties at any time through the file menu.

To change the description of a Program Group,

1. Minimize Mygroup so that it is an icon.
2. Click on the Mygroup icon (not the description).
3. Choose File and Properties from the Program Manager menu.
4. Type a new description: **Tasks**
5. Click on OK.

To change the icon for a Program Item,

1. Open the Tasks group window.
2. Click on the Logfile icon to make it active.
3. Choose File and Properties from the Program Manager menu.
4. Click on the Change Icon command button (see Figure 10-6).

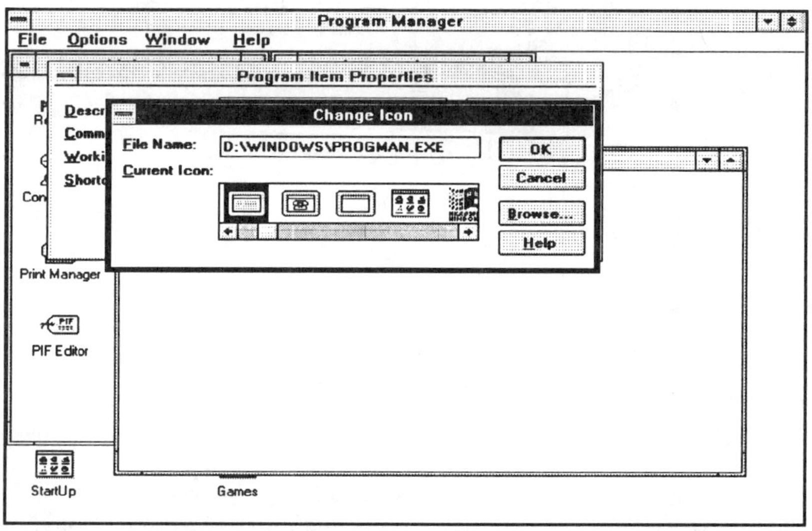

Figure 10-6: *Changing to a Different Icon*

5. At the dialog box, click on Browse.
6. From the filelist of icons, double-click on a file of your choice. If you double-click on an **.exe** file, a new icon will appear.

If you double-click on a **.dll** file, you will get a display of icons to choose from.
If you are not happy with the resulting icon, repeat the procedure as many times as necessary.

7. Click on OK.

Deleting Program Items and Groups

If you have no need for a program item and/or group, you can easily delete it.

To delete a program item,

1. Make sure the Tasks group window is active.
2. Click on the Notepad icon to make it active.
3. Press **DELETE** (or choose File and Delete from the Program Manager menu.)
4. Read the Delete Confirmation box and answer **Yes** if the information is correct.
5. Delete the other two icons in the group in the same manner.

To delete a program group,

1. Make sure the Tasks group window is still active.
2. The group must be empty of icons. Delete any that remain.
3. Press **DELETE** (or choose File and Delete from the Program Manager menu).
   If the Confirm box has the correct information,
4. Confirm the deletion by answering **Yes**.

Using the Startup Group

When Windows 3.1 is installed, a program group called Startup will be included. The Startup group will be empty until you add one or more program items to it. The items added to the Startup group will automatically open when Windows is started. If there are certain applications or documents you *always* want to run when you start Windows, this is the group window where they belong.

You may add program items to the Startup group just as you add them to other program groups. DO NOT make any changes to the startup group if you are using a lab computer.

Adding Applications from the Hard Disk

Windows enables you to bring applications from your hard disk into the Windows environment, whether or not you have a program group ready to receive these applications. This topic will be covered in Appendix C.

Closing Exercise

1. Delete any icons you have added to the Startup group.
2. Delete any other programs items or groups you have added that remain.
3. Close Windows.

Review Exercises

1. Open Windows.
2. Create a program group called Daily.
3. Use File Properties to add the following program items to your group: Write, Paintbrush, Calculator, Clock, Mycal (from your Student Data disk), and File Manager. **WARNING! DO NOT MOVE the program items from other windows!**
4. Change the name of the Paintbrush icon to Drawing and the name of your calendar icon to Appts.
5. Move the clock from your new group to the Startup group. Then delete the clock from the startup group.
6. Delete Write from your new group.
7. Use File Properties to add the file **a:\inquiry2.wri** or **b:\inquiry.wri** to your new program group.
8. Double-click on **INQUIRY2**. What program is activated?
9. Change the name of your program group to Tasks.
10. Delete all the program items from Tasks.
11. Delete the program group.

11

Creating Special Links Between Applications

The objectives of this lesson are to

- Create an embedded object
- Create linked objects
- Embed an object package in a document

In Lesson 7 we learned to copy and move data between Windows applications. Windows 3.1 offers you additional, powerful ways to exchange and connect information between files. The methods we will discuss in this lesson are embedding objects, linking objects, and packaging objects.

What Is an Object?

Any document or part of a document created in Windows can be used as an object. An object can be a drawing, a paragraph or more of text, part of a spreadsheet—in other words, just about any information entity you treat as a unit. The advantage of working with data in the form of an object rather than as data you have merely selected becomes apparent when you want to edit or update it.

Object linking, embedding, and packaging are not limited to the applications included with Windows 3.1. Other Windows applications, including Microsoft Excel and Word for Windows, support these functions. If you are not sure if an application supports linking and embedding, check the documentation for that application.

In all of these methods:

- The object is created in the *source* application.
- The object is embedded into the *destination* application (also known as the *client* application).

What Is Object Embedding?

Object embedding enables you to take an object created in one application and *embed* or place it into another application. When an object is embedded, it can be edited more quickly and easily than when it is copied or moved.

To edit an object that has been embedded in a different application, double-click on it. Windows will automatically return you to the source application (where the object was created). You can then edit or change the object in its own application. Click again to *update* the object in the destination application, but not, however, in the source application. The editing process updates only the destination, *not* the source.

In this part of our lesson, we will use Windows Paintbrush as the source application and Windows Write as the destination application. Windows Paintbrush is an application used for drawing pictures and symbols. We will *embed* an object created in Paintbrush into a Write document.

Note: Before you begin this lesson, make sure your Student Data disk has been inserted into the correct drive.

Note: The exercises using Paintbrush will not work if you have only the minimum amount of memory (RAM) recommended by Microsoft for running Windows (see Introduction.) Paintbrush saves files as bit-mapped images (.bmp). These files are large and require a great deal of memory. Your PC should have at least 2 megabytes of RAM to work with Paintbrush.

To embed an object in Windows Write,

1. Open Windows and open the Accessories window.
2. Open Write and maximize its window (not required, but recommended).
3. Type the following:

   Here is a simple drawing created in Windows Paintbrush:

4. Press ENTER three times to bring your cursor to the point where the drawing will appear.
5. Choose Edit and Insert Object from the menu (see Figure 11-1). At the dialog box, you will see a list of applications that support object linking and embedding. This list is generated by Windows based upon the software installed on your computer. Thus, your list may look different from the one in Figure 11-1.
6. Scroll the list and double-click on Paintbrush Picture.
   The Paintbrush application will open. Since we have not learned to use Paintbrush, we will not create a drawing, but instead will use one that has been saved on your Student Data disk.

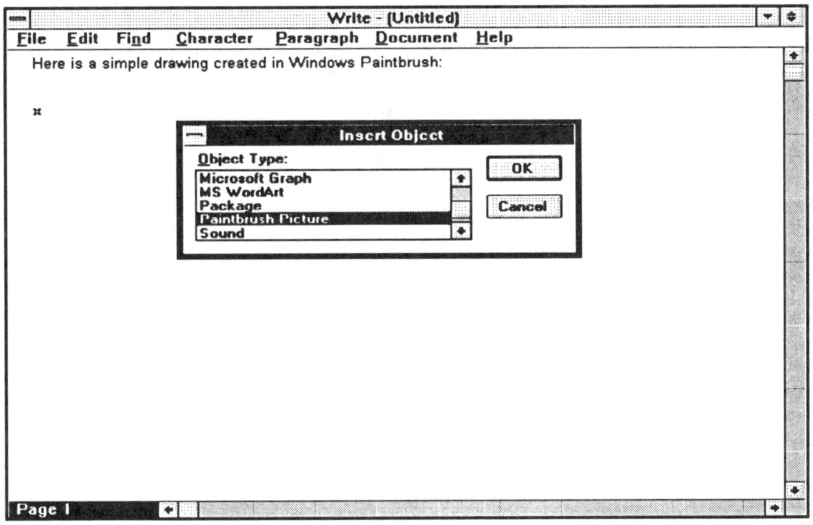

Figure 11-1: *Embedding an Object*

7. Maximize the Paintbrush screen.
8. At the Paintbrush menu, choose Edit and Paste From.
9. Select the drive in which your Student Data disk has been inserted.
10. Click on the file house.bmp and click on OK. Because the file is so large, it will take a long time to retrieve from your floppy disk.
11. Choose File and Update to embed the drawing in Write.
12. Choose File and Exit & Return To... in order to leave Paintbrush.

Paintbrush will close and you will return to Write. Scroll upward in Write or press CTRL+HOME to see the drawing that has been embedded.

Once the object has been embedded, it is part of the destination document. It can be printed and saved like any other part of the document. To edit the object, use the source application.

To Edit an embedded object,

1. Double-click on any part of the drawing to return to Paintbrush. Once we have returned to the Paintbrush screen, you can see the drawing ready to be edited. Since we have not learned to use Paintbrush, we will make only a simple change.
2. Maximize the Paintbrush window.
3. Click on the color green at the bottom of the Paintbrush screen.

Note: If you have a color monitor and Paintbrush is not displaying colors, choose Options and Image Attributes at the menu. Click on Colors at the Image Attributes dialog box and then click on OK.

4. Click on the **Paintroller** tool (left column, fourth from the top) to select it.
5. Click on each section of the house to paint it green.
   Do not save the document in Paintbrush. The advantage of embedding the house in Write is that you can keep editing it in Paintbrush, without having to change the Paintbrush file.
6. Choose File and Update.
   This will update the image in your Write document. Remember, you cannot edit the drawing in Write. If you had merely copied the house to Write and not embedded it, you would have had to select it and move it to Paintbrush, edit it in Paintbrush, and finally select and move it back to Write.
7. Choose File and Exit & Return To...
8. Click on a blank part of the Write screen to deselect the object.
9. Save the Write drawing as **greenhse** and exit from Write.

What Is Object Linking?

When an object is *embedded*, you can automatically return to the source application for editing and updating. In object *linking*, the same object exists in both the source and one or more destination documents, and an open link exists between the files. When you edit the object in the source, the destination(s) are automatically updated. This is particularly useful when you need to keep duplicate information in different files. After linking the objects, you need to enter the data only once, and your linked files will always contain consistent information.

In this section, we will again use Paintbrush as our source and Write as our destination.

To link an object,

1. Open Write and maximize it.
2. Open Paintbrush and maximize it.
3. At Paintbrush, choose File Open. Select the drive containing your Student Data disk and open the document named **wheel.bmp**.
4. Click on the *right* Scissors tool (top of the second column).
5. Move your mouse pointer above and to the right of the picture.
6. Click and drag the mouse across the picture to draw a box around it (see Figure 11-2).
7. Choose Edit and Copy.
8. Open the Control Menu and use the Task List to switch to Windows Write.
9. Choose Edit and Paste Link to paste the object into Write and also create a link to Paintbrush.
10. In Write, save the document as **wheelink**.
11. Do not exit from Write, unless you are not going on to the next exercise.

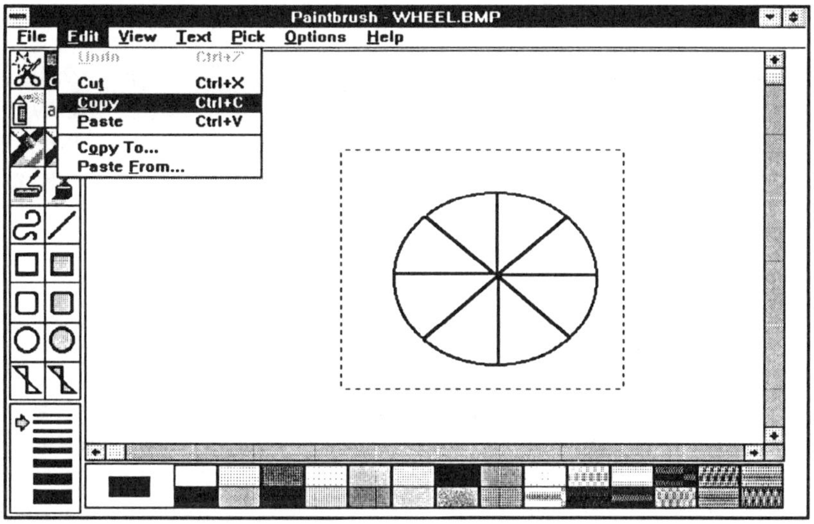

Figure 11-2: *Preparing to Link Objects*

The same object (the drawing) now exists in two different applications and the drawings are linked.

To edit a linked object,

1. Switch back to Paintbrush and make sure that **wheel.bmp** is open.
2. Click on the color blue at the bottom of the screen.
3. Click on the Paintroller tool.
4. Click on the *rim* of the wheel to change the background color.
5. Switch back to Write.
   The background has been repainted here too! As long as the link remains open, any change to the source file will automatically be updated in the destination.
6. Use File Save to save the file again in Write. Do not save the file in Paintbrush.
7. Close both Write and Paintbrush.

Embedding an Object Package in a Document

A third way to use the power of embedded objects is to embed them as *packages*. A package appears as an icon in your document and contains the text or picture you choose. To open the package, activate the icon by clicking on it. To package an object and embed it in a document, use the **Object Packager**, which is found in the Accessories window.

The advantage of packaging an object is that the information contained in the package may be needed in some situations and not in others. The package is placed in the document, represented by the icon, and can be opened only when necessary. When it is not needed it remains an icon, taking up little space. This feature is used by Windows itself when creating the *definition terms* found on Help screens. You can probably think of other instances when you have seen this technique used.

There are two Write documents on your Student Data disk, named **listing.wri** and **explain.wri**. **Listing** contains a list of the Windows accessories, and **explain** describes the features of each. We are going to use the Object Packager to insert explain into list as a package.

To create an Object Package,

1. Switch to the Program Manager (if necessary) and open the Accessories window.
2. Open the Object Packager by double-clicking.
   The Object Packager contains two windows. The Content window will contain the name of the file being packaged. The Appearance window will contain the icon used to represent the package (see Figure 11-3).

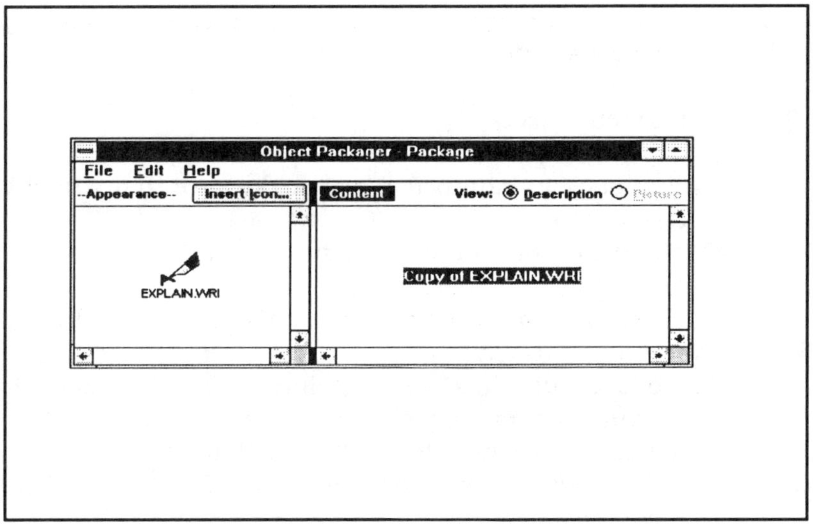

Figure 11-3: The Object Packager

3. Click on the word **Content** to make that window active.
4. At the menu, choose File and Import.
5. Select the drive containing your Student Data disk.
6. Double-click on the file named **explain.wri**.

The filename will appear in the Content window and an icon will appear in the Appearance window. The icon will match the application in which the file was created.

To embed the package in a document,

1. At the menu, choose Edit and Copy Package.

2. Leave the Object Packager open. Use the control menu to switch to Write or, if Write is not open, switch to the Program Manager and open Write.
3. Open the document titled **Listing** (remember to switch to the drive containing your Student Data disk).
4. Move your cursor two lines above the first item on the list (Calculator).
5. Choose Edit and Paste.
   The package will appear at your cursor's location (see Figure 11-4). To open the package, double-click on its icon. Close the window that contains the package as you would any other window.

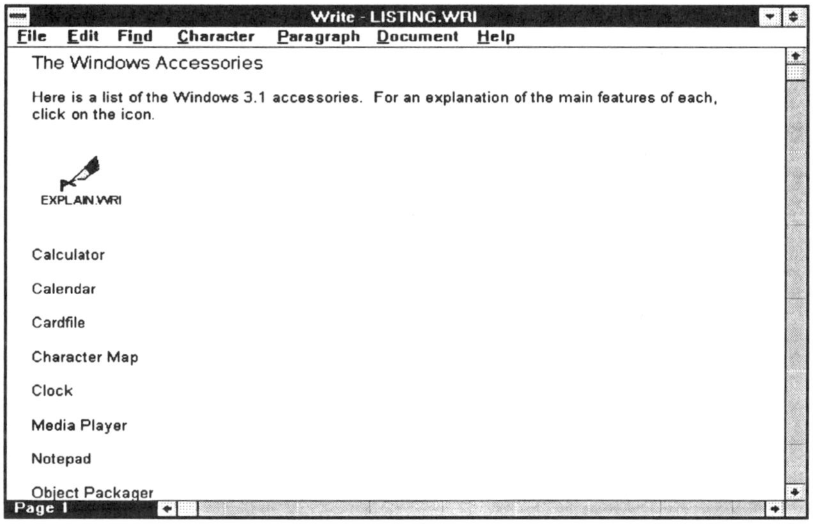

Figure 11-4: *An Object Package in a Document*

6. Close the Object Packager window from the Task List by pressing CTRL-ESC to reach the Task List, clicking on Object Packager and clicking on END TASK.
7. Use File Save to save the document, including the icon, as **listing2**.
8. Close Write.
9. Close Windows.

Review Exercises

1. A. Open Paintbrush and Write.
   B. From Write, choose Edit and Insert Object. Then, choose Paintbrush Picture.
   C. From Paintbrush, use Edit and Paste From to embed the drawing called **sea.bmp** into Write (hint: **sea.bmp** is on your hard drive, so *do not* change to the drive containing your Student Data disk). If you do not have **sea.bmp**, use any **.bmp** file from your hard drive.

D. Choose File Update to embed the drawing in Write and File Exit & Return To...to close Paintbrush.

E. In Write, view the drawing and then double-click on it to edit the drawing.

F. In Paintbrush, change the background color of the drawing, following the instructions in the first section of this lesson. *Do not* save the drawing in Paintbrush. Update the drawing and exit from Paintbrush.

G. Close Write without saving the drawing.

2. A. Open Paintbrush and maximize it. Open the file **house.bmp**, which you used earlier in this lesson.

B. From Paintbrush, select and copy the picture to Write, choosing Paste Link.

C. Switch back to Paintbrush and change the color of the design. Return to Write and check that the change has taken effect in the linked file also.

D. *Do not* save the file in either Paintbrush or Write. Close both applications.

3. A. In Windows Write, begin a new document and write a description of a short project you would like to create in Windows. Save the document as **project**.

B. Begin another new document in Write and record the steps you would need to follow to create your project. Save this document as **instruct**.

C. Embed the second document as an object package icon at the end of **project.** Insert a blank line before the icon and on the line, type: **For instructions on how to create this project, double-click on the icon**.

APPENDIX

Appendix A
Suggested Projects

1. Create your own Windows cardfile.
   A. Include names, addresses, telephone numbers, and other information of your choice.
   B. Change to List View and print your list of cards.
   C. Save your cardfile. If you are not working on your own PC, save the file on a floppy disk.

2. Use the Windows calendar to record your appointments.
   A. Include also upcoming holidays, test and assignment dates for this course, and special reminders.
   B. Print all your appointments for the current week.
   C. Save your calendar. If you are not working on your own PC, save the file on a floppy disk.

3. Create a special program group of your own.
   A. Include icons for the documents, reports, and applications you regularly work with.
   B. If you are not working on your own PC, delete the group before you leave Windows.

4. Choose a wallpaper or pattern you like for the Desktop.
   A. Customize a screen saver.
   B. Adjust the cursor speed, granularity, and border width to suit your preferences.
   C. If you are not working on your own PC, return to former settings before you leave Windows.

5. Create your own personal Help document in Windows Write, including pop-up help windows.

A. Create a document in Windows Write describing the commands or procedures you find difficult.

B. After you have described each command or procedure in general terms, save the document.

C. Create a document in Write for *each* of the commands or procedures you described, giving complete, detailed instructions. Save each set of instructions as a separate file.

D. Use the Object Packager to create an icon for each of these documents.

E. Embed each icon in your original document immediately following the command or procedure it refers to.

F. Add instructions to the original document, which tell the user to double-click on any icon to display instructions for carrying out that command or procedure.

APPENDIX

Appendix B
Installing Windows and Printing in Windows

1. Installing Windows

As long as you have sufficient room on your hard drive, installing Windows is easy. Once you begin the procedure by typing a simple command, you need only follow the directions on the screen.

You can install Windows using Express setup or Custom Setup:

> **Express** setup is recommended by Microsoft for most users. With this method, Windows makes many of your decisions for you, based on the preferences of thousands of surveyed users. It also takes into account your own hardware and software. Express setup is quick and easy to use.
>
> **Custom** setup is recommended for the user who is not happy with the standard Windows settings and knows how to select a different configuration.

To begin Windows setup (for both Express and Custom),

1. Insert Microsoft Windows 3.1 **Disk 1** into a floppy drive on your computer.
2. Change the active drive to that floppy drive (type **a:** or **b:** and press **ENTER**.)
3. Type the word **setup**.
4. Press **ENTER**.
5. Follow directions as they appear on your screen.

As Setup begins, Windows searches your hard drive, looking for earlier versions of Windows. It also looks for other installed software that has trouble working with Windows, and may display a warning message if it finds such applications.

If you have an earlier version of Windows installed, Windows will ask you if you want to overwrite that version with Windows 3.1 or instead keep both versions in separate directories. Windows recommends that users overwrite the old version of Windows. Doing so will enable you to keep your old program groups and document files, and many of your settings. Other experts feel, however, that it is better to keep versions 3.0 and 3.1 separate. These experts advise users who need only one version of Windows to first back up document files saved with version 3.0 onto floppy disks and then to erase 3.0 entirely. Only after this procedure should 3.1 be installed.

If you do not have enough room on your hard disk to install the complete Windows 3.1, you can choose to install only certain parts of the program. Again, Windows will guide you in making your choices.

2. Printing in Windows 3.1

The printing process has been greatly improved in the update from Windows Version 3.0 to 3.1. There are three ways in which you, the user, can troubleshoot the printing process:

If Your Problem Is...	Use the...	Features
Setting Up Printers	**Printers Icon**	The Printers icon in the Control Panel (found in the Main program group), is used to add and remove printers, set default printers, and switch between Network and personal printers. When you add or remove a printer, the change will be reflected throughout the Windows environment.
Print Job Starts but does not Finish	**Print Manager**	The Print Manager is an icon in the Main program group. It controls all jobs that have been sent to the printer. If other documents are waiting to print, it will control the queue, or waiting line. If there is a printing problem, the Print Manager will document the problem in a message. You can use the Print Manager to temporarily pause your print job, resume it when you are ready, or delete the job from the print queue.
Doesn't Print	**File Print Setup**	Each application that allows you to print a document has a Print Setup command in its File menu. This is the easiest way to activate a printer or change from one installed printer to another.

Printers are set up in Windows during installation. To make changes to your current setup, double-click the Printers icon in the Control

Panel. At the Printers dialog box, you will see a list of installed printers. One printer will be listed as the default printer. Use this dialog box to add and remove printers from your setup. There is also a checkbox labeled **Use Print Manager**. Make sure this box is checked so that the Print Manager will operate.

When the box is checked, the Print Manager will automatically open when there is a printing problem. You will see its icon appear at the bottom of the desktop, unless a window has been maximized, in which case it will be open but not visible. If the Print Manager icon is covered by a window, switch to it through the Task List.

The Print Manager will tell you the nature of your printing problem. When you have corrected the problem, the print job will resume. The Print Manager closes automatically when there are no jobs printing, and its icon disappears from the desktop.

There are times when you may not want the Print Manager to control your printing, for example when you are printing in a non-Windows application. For those instances, return to the Printers dialog box and uncheck the Print Manager checkbox.

Whenever you are printing, you can change to a different installed printer by using the File menu's **Print Setup** command. If you send a document to the printer and nothing happens, use this command to make sure that the right printer is active. You can also click on Print Setup *before* you print, to make sure that the correct printer has been selected and the options are set to your liking.

APPENDIX

Appendix C
Using Non-Windows Applications

What are Non-Windows Applications?

Non-Windows applications are programs that are designed to run in the DOS environment, not the Windows environment. Nonetheless, with sufficient memory you can run these applications under Windows, and doing so offers you several advantages:

- In 386 Enhanced Mode, the non-Windows application can be run in a window, which can be moved and sized.
- In 386 Enhanced Mode, you can run more than one task at a time, including both Windows and non-Windows applications.
- Information can be copied and moved between Windows and non-Windows applications by using the Clipboard.

Information needed for Windows to run each non-Windows application is saved in a *program information file*, known as a *PIF* file. Windows provides a PIF file for each common non-Windows application. It also provides a default PIF file that will work for most applications. You can use one of the existing PIF files, or create one to specify settings that will help your application run better. You will find instructions for working with PIF files later in this Appendix.

Adding Non-Windows Applications to the Windows Environment

When you install Windows, you can create a separate program group for your non-Windows applications. You can add to or remove applications from this group exactly as you would any other group. Even when Windows is already installed, you can add non-Windows applications to your group by selecting them directly from the hard disk.

Windows allows you to bring applications from your hard disk into the Windows environment, whether or not you have Program Groups ready to receive these applications. The Windows **Set-up** icon in the Main group provides an Option called **Set-up Applications**, which will search the drives you request and provide a list of both Windows and non-Windows applications it finds. You can choose to add these applications to your program groups.

If program groups named **Windows Applications** and **Non-Windows Applications** are already set up, Windows will place the applications you select into these groups, but if they do not exist, Windows will create these groups for you as part of the Set-up Applications command. Windows recognizes which applications belong in the Windows Applications program group, and which applications belong in the Non-Windows program group.

To add applications through Windows Set-up,

- Open the **Main** group window.
- Double-Click on **Windows Set-up**.
- Choose **Options** and click on **Set-up Applications**.
- To have Windows search all hard drives, choose **OK**.
- When the Set-up Applications dialog box appears, select each application you wish to add to Windows and click on **Add**.
- CLICK on **OK**.
- Close the **Set-up** window. The applications you have selected are now part of the Windows environment. Windows will provide you with an icon for each non-Windows application.

To start a Non-Windows application,

- Double-click on the icon for the application.
- Windows will automatically search for the PIF file that belongs to the application. If you have created your own PIF file or edited the existing PIF file, make sure that it has the same name as the file that runs the application. For example, if your application is started by a file named **wp.exe**, your PIF file should be **wp.pif**. If the PIF filename is not correct, Windows will not be able to locate it and will not run the application.

Running a Non-Windows Application in a Window

When you are running in Windows 386 Enhanced Mode, you can bring a non-Windows application into a window. In addition to being able to move and size the window, you can use the mouse with your application. You can move and copy data from one application into another Windows or non-Windows application (for example, you can copy part of a Lotus spreadsheet into a WordPerfect document). In effect, you are treating the application like a Windows application.

To see if Windows is running in enhanced mode,

- From the Program Manager, choose **Help**.
- Choose **About Program Manager**.
- The current mode will be listed near the bottom of the dialog box.
- If you have a 386 model computer and 2 megabytes or more of memory, you can make sure that Windows runs in 386 Enhanced Mode by typing **win /e** at the DOS prompt when you start Windows.

When you start a non-Windows application, it may run in a full-screen (maximized) version. To bring it into a window, press **ALT+ENTER**. You can set the PIF file for the application so that it will always run in a window. Instructions for that follow later in this Appendix.

The Non-Windows Control Menu

Once your non-Windows application is brought into a window, it will have its own control menu. This menu is similar to that of Windows applications, with three additions:

- **Edit** — Allows you to transfer data to other applications, regardless of whether they are Windows applications, by letting you select text, copy, paste, and scroll.
- **Settings** — Lets you control the display, multitasking, and priority of your application.
- **Fonts** — Lets you change fonts. You can also change fonts within the application.

The **Edit** menu allows you to use the Windows Clipboard to copy data to other Windows and non-Windows applications.

To transfer data to another application,

- Open the Control menu of the non-Windows application.
- Choose **Edit Mark**.
- Select the data you wish to copy with your mouse.
- Press the *right* mouse button to copy the data to the Clipboard. This is one of the few instances where the right mouse button is used.
- If you are copying to a Windows application, follow the normal procedure for that application.
- If you are copying to a non-Windows application, use the following directions:

To receive data from another application,

- Open the application and bring it into a window.
- Move the cursor to the point where you want to place the copied data.
- Open the control menu of the non-Windows application.
- Choose **Edit Paste**.

The **Settings** command on the non-Windows control menu leads to a dialog box that offers you several options for running your non-Windows application.

Display lets you choose whether your application will run in a window or in a full-screen version. If you choose **Full Screen**, the application will switch to a full screen as soon as you click on **OK**, and the Control menu will disappear. However, you are not forced to remain in a full-screen display. By pressing **ALT+ENTER** you can return the application to a window and regain the commands it offers.

Tasking lets you tell Windows how to handle the current application when you are also working in other applications. It can be used when Windows will be working in more than one application at a time (multitasking). Either or both options may be selected.

Exclusive makes the current application the *only* non-Windows application that will run. Other non-Windows applications will be suspended, but Windows applications can continue to run.

Background lets the application continue to run in the background while you continue to process other Windows and non-Windows applications. However, if another application has the **Exclusive** setting checked, this second application will not run.

Priority lets you control how much CPU time the current application will receive in a multitasking situation. The more CPU time an application receives relative to another application, the faster it will be processed.

Foreground controls the percentage of CPU time your application will receive when it is the *active* application.

Background controls the percentage of CPU time your application will receive when it is *not* the active application. Your application will not receive *any* CPU time, however, unless you allow it to run in the background by checking that box in the **Tasking** options.

Terminate is not for normal use. When you are working in a non-windows application, exit in the usual procedure for that application. If this does not work, then you may use the **Terminate** command. Occasionally, using the **Terminate** command may cause you to lose some data; therefore, it should be used only as a last resort.

Creating a PIF File

Most standard applications already contain a PIF file on the Windows installation disk. However, sometimes it is necessary to create your own PIF file for running a non-Windows application. Once you are familiar with PIF files you may want to edit existing ones to run your non-Windows applications more efficiently.

To create a PIF file for an application,

- Start the **PIF Editor** from the Main program group window.
- The PIF parameter window that is displayed is the one for the current mode. If you are setting parameters to run a non-Windows application when you are running Windows in a different mode, use the Mode Menu to select that mode.
- Fill in the window by defining the parameters (described below).
- Save the file by using the **Save As** option in the **File** Menu. Each PIF file must have a different name (see Filename, below).
- **Close** the editor by double-clicking on its control menu.
- You can create multiple PIF files for an application. If you do, always start the program by clicking or selecting the correct PIF filename, not the application name. In this way, you know which PIF file is being used. If you

click on the program name, the PIF file that most closely resembles the program name will be used.

The PIF editor is a Windows application that can be used to create or modify existing PIF files. Your screen may have fewer or different parameters, depending on which mode Windows is operating in. The most important file parameters are defined below:

PIF File Parameters

Program Filename	The program name *must* include the name of the file that starts the application, including the complete path *and* extension. To execute a program, the extension must be **.com** or **.exe**. To start a program from a batch file, the extension **.bat** must be included.
Window Title	This is the name that will be used for the program's icon when the program is minimized. Keep the name short because the space for the icon is small.
Optional Parameters	Windows can start a program using any start-up options available in the program. This includes filenames, letters, or numbers, up to 62 characters. Leave a space between the program name and document name. Make sure you include the directory for the document if it is different.
Start-up Directory	This entry defines the directory that Windows should be in when running the program.
Video Memory	Windows remembers the memory required for displaying each application. If you select **text** the program will run only in text mode. This minimizes the amount of memory used. If you select **Low Graphics**, you will use about 32K of memory and your screen will resemble CGA format. If you select **High Graphics**, you will use about 128K of memory and your screen will resemble VGA format.
Memory Req.	This entry specifies the amount of memory to start the application. The specification should be in kilobytes and is generally set at 128K.
KB Desired	This will set a maximum amount of memory that an application may use.

EMS Memory	Windows does not use *expanded* memory, but instead simulates it for applications that require it. Use these parameters to specify EMS required to start the application and the desired maximum amount of EMS to be used by the application.
XMS Memory	These settings specify the amount of *extended* memory required to start an application and the desired maximum amount of XMS to be used by the application.
Display Usage	This option lets you control whether the application will begin in a full-screen or window version.
Execution	This option controls whether the application can run in the background while another application is being processed and whether other non-Windows applications must be suspended when this application is active.
Close Window on Exit	This box is usually checked. However, if you want Windows to leave output on the screen after you close the application, do not check the box.
Advanced	These options give closer control over how your non-Windows application runs. For further information, see your Windows documentation.

APPENDIX

Appendix D
Shortcut Keys

Windows *can* be used without a mouse. To use the keyboard efficiently, this table of shortcut keys will serve as a reference:

KEYS	FUNCTION
APPLICATION WINDOW SHORTCUTS	
ALT+ESC	Switches to the next application window or icon, activating each one.
ALT+TAB	Switches to the next application window, restoring applications running as icons. The last window restored becomes the active window.
CTRL+ESC	Opens the Task List
ALT+SPACEBAR	Opens the control menu of an application
ALT+F4	Closes any application window
ALT+ENTER	Switches a non-Windows application between fullscreen and window presentation
DOCUMENT WINDOW SHORTCUTS	
CTRL+TAB or CTRL+F6	Switches to the next document window or icon
CTRL+F4	Closes a document window

ALT+HYPHEN	Opens the control menu of a document window
MENU SHORTCUTS	
ALT	Activates and de-activates the menu bar
Underlined Letter	Chooses a menu or menu command
ENTER	Chooses a menu or menu command
ESCAPE	Cancels a selected menu
ARROW KEYS	Moves you around menu choices
DIALOG BOX SHORTCUTS	
TAB	Moves around options in a dialog box
SHIFT+TAB	Moves among options in a dialog box in reverse order
SPACEBAR	Selects or cancels a selection
ARROW KEYS	Moves among choices within a single option
ESCAPE	Cancels a dialog box
ALT+UNDER-LINED LETTER	Moves to the option whose letter you typed. Sometimes selects or deselects an option.

INDEX